The Emotional Impact of Being Scammed and How to Recover

The Emotional Impact of Being Scammed and How to Recover

By Cathy Wilson, LPC ACS

Copyright © 2021 Cathy Wilson. All rights reserved. No part of this book may be reproduced or used in any manner without written permission of the copyright owner except for the use of quotations in a book review. For more information, please contact cw@lifepathscounseling.com.

Copyediting by Joanna B. Brewer, joannabbrewer.com

Praise for "The Emotional Impact of Being Scammed and How to Recover"

"Thank you Cathy for providing such a valuable resource on an important topic that isn't discussed enough. I appreciate your compassionate, yet direct, style that will surely allow readers to begin to process their experiences, validate their emotions, and find a path forward in the healing process. The book provides concrete and helpful techniques and tools that offer a way to decrease shame and increase self-kindness.

Cathy has a talent for creating a feeling of connection through her writing, as though she were walking beside the reader on the journey forward. I highly recommend that anyone who is a survivor of the trauma of being scammed read this informative and helpful book. If you have a loved one who has been scammed this is for you as well. I am excited to be able to recommend this book to people both in my professional and personal worlds."

Michelle Lefco-Rockey, Licensed Clinical Social Worker

Creekside Collaborative Therapy, Centennial, Colorado

"This book is a fantastic resource for anyone who has been the victim of a scam. It validates the emotional toll and describes in detail what people who have been on the receiving end of a scam might encounter emotionally. It also provides very reassuring and practical suggestions for healing. It is well written, easy to understand, and chock full of very valuable information. I know it will provide tremendous comfort and reassurance for anyone who has been the victim of a scam."

Suzanne Smith, LCSW

Align Counseling Center, https://www.aligncc.com

"Fraud victims often suffer from emotional distress and find it hard to move on from the experience. They may feel like they have nobody to talk to about it, so they suffer in silence.

They find themselves faced with a multitude of negative and debilitating emotions, ranging from shame to despair, any of which can lead them down a very dark hole.

It is easy to feel overwhelmed by the sense of loss and pain.

Those who have been ripped off by a scam have an emotional wound that is very real and very deep. The thought that they have been taken in, and may have even been responsible for being scammed, can be frightening and confusing.

This book is a much-needed resource for anyone who has been the victim of fraud, whether it be a one-time incident or long-term abuse. It provides detailed information and expert opinion on how to recover emotionally from the harmful impact of fraud and scams.

As an authority on these types of crimes, I feel this book can help survivors overcome the emotional fallout of fraud and get on a positive path to recovery."

Les Henderson, Author of *Crimes of Persuasion: Schemes, Scams, Frauds*

https://www.crimes-of-persuasion.com/

"What Cathy has done with this book is to finally offer a sense of relief for those who were targeted by a scammer. In my work as a trauma therapist, I often see people plagued with self-blame for events that were not of their own doing, events that leave the survivor feeling tainted, shamed, and scarred.

The Emotional Impact of Being Scammed and How to Recover can help the survivor of a scam understand where the true responsibilities lie, undermining and deconstructing the internal chorus of shame and blame, while offering a path towards empowerment and healing. I am so glad this much-needed resource is finally available."

Eric J. Blommel, MA, NCC, MFTC

Improve Counseling, LLC, improvecounseling.com, Relationship and Trauma Therapist

"Cathy Wilson has written what may be the first book of its kind – one that is written by a mental health professional specifically for crime victims who have been scammed, and their loved ones.

Wilson is quickly earning her global reputation as the sole authority on the remedial work of psychological repair that is often needed to help victims of fraud, identity theft, and scams begin to reconstruct their emotional lives and regain their sense of direction and confidence to move forward.

For those individuals who have been scammed, those who love them, and those who work with them, this is a must-read!"

Tamara G. Suttle, M.Ed, LPC, ACS

Private Practice from the Inside Out

https://www.TamaraSuttle.com

"Cathy Wilson, a mental health professional and respected expert in her field, takes her readers into the not-often-talked-about yet highly harmful impact that victims of scam crimes endure.

Cathy educates her readers about different types of scams, the varied emotions a victim may experience (hint: shame, embarrassment, feelings of stupidity to name a few), and what a person can do to heal the complexities of this psychological injury. Cathy includes practical skills and tools, resources, and even a chapter for family and friends of victims of scam crimes so her readers can move toward regaining a sense of confidence and trust in others and, more importantly, themselves- leading to wholeness and wellness.

The Emotional Impact of Being Scammed and How to Recover is the go-to resource for anyone impacted directly or indirectly by a scam crime, and is essential reading for professionals who work with this population!"

Barbara Sheehan-Zeidler, MA, LPC, EMDRIA Approved Consultant

Creative and Caring Counseling

https://www.CreativeAndCaringCounseling.com

"I appreciate how Cathy Wilson was able to clearly identify the challenges that so many survivors of scams have experienced. Cathy has a beautiful way of providing information and understanding in a non-judgmental and compassionate way. She clearly describes the pain, the shame, and the guilt these survivors experience and allows them to know that they are not alone in their pain. Cathy provides concrete skills to help survivors and their loved ones understand, process, and move past the devastating impacts of being scammed. She integrates multiple types of tools to help survivors be able to identify possible future scammers, protect themselves, and heal from their past scams.

This is an essential resource for any person who has been scammed, has a friend or family member who is a survivor of a scam, and for anyone wanting ways to protect themselves from being scammed. I am excited to finally be able to have a resource to recommend to my patients who have found themselves survivors of scams."

Tonya McFarland, PsyD, LP, CEDS

Trusted Therapy

https://www.TrustedTherapy.com

Dedication

To every person who has been the survivor of a scam or fraud, I hope that you find healing in whatever form you need. I salute your courage and resilience with all of my heart.

Table of Contents

PRAISE FOR "THE EMOTIONAL IMPACT OF BEING SCAMMED AND HOW TO RECOVER"	I
DEDICATION	V
DISCLAIMER	XIII
INTRODUCTION	XV
HOW TO USE THIS BOOK	XVII
TYPES OF SCAMS	XX
PART 1 – THE EMOTIONAL IMPACT OF BEING SCAMMED	**1**
CHAPTER 1: THE IMPACT ON EMOTIONS AND THOUGHTS	**3**
SHAME	4
ANGER	4
GRIEF AND LOSS	5
EMBARRASSMENT	8

Guilt	9
Anxiety and Fear	9
Depression	10
Disbelief and Shock	11
Damaged Self-Worth	11
What Can You Do to Feel Better?	12
Chapter 2: The Impact on Relationships	**15**
Loss of Trust in Others	15
Your Partner Feels Betrayed	16
Taking Your Emotions Out on Others	16
Isolation and Withdrawing	17
Ruminating and Not Getting "Over It"	17
Changed View of Relationships	18
Separating the Fictitious Person from the Criminal	18
What Can You Do to Feel Better?	19
Chapter 3: The Impact on Identity	**21**
Lack of Trust in Yourself and Self-Doubt	21
Lack of Security in the World	22

BELIEFS ABOUT SELF, OTHERS, AND THE WORLD	22
YOU ARE NOT STUPID	23
WHAT CAN YOU DO TO FEEL BETTER?	23
PART 2 – HOW DID THIS HAPPEN?	**25**
CHAPTER 4: HUMANS ARE NOT PERFECT	27
CHAPTER 5: FORMS OF MANIPULATION	31
CHAPTER 6: PSYCHOLOGICAL BIASES	43
CHAPTER 7: COGNITIVE DISTORTIONS	49
CHAPTER 8: PERSUASION TECHNIQUES	53
PART 3 – HEALING AND RECOVERY	**57**
CHAPTER 9: SELF-CARE	59
TAKE CARE OF YOUR PHYSICAL BODY	60
DON'T OVERDO IT - KNOW YOUR LIMITS	60
DO THINGS YOU ENJOY AND THAT REPLENISH YOUR ENERGY	61
BOUNDARIES	66
CHAPTER 10: PROTECTING YOURSELF IN THE FUTURE	69
EDUCATE YOURSELF	69
PRACTICE RECOGNIZING FORMS OF MANIPULATION, PSYCHOLOGICAL BIASES, COGNITIVE DISTORTIONS, AND PERSUASION TECHNIQUES	70

REPORT THE CRIME	71
RESPONDING WHEN YOU THINK IT IS ANOTHER SCAM	71
HOLDING ENERGETIC BOUNDARIES	75
CHAPTER 11: HEALING	**87**
CHANGE IN THOUGHT/EMOTION SKILLS	88
CONCEPTS TO EXPLORE	97
ACTIONS	102
CHAPTER 12: FOR FAMILY AND FRIENDS	**111**
LISTEN AND EMPATHIZE WITHOUT JUDGEMENT	111
DON'T SAY…	112
REMIND YOUR LOVED ONE FREQUENTLY: "YOU ARE NOT STUPID"	112
FOCUS ON WHAT <u>CAN</u> BE DONE	113
ENCOURAGE YOUR LOVED ONE TO FORGIVE THEMSELVES	114
REMEMBER THESE FACTORS	114
CHAPTER 13: CONCLUDING THOUGHTS	**117**
APPENDIX A: TYPES OF SCAMS	**119**
APPENDIX B: RESOURCES	**121**
SUPPORT GROUPS:	121

LAW ENFORCEMENT/CRIME VICTIM SUPPORT:	122
BOOKS/WEBSITES:	123
REFERENCES	**125**
ABOUT CATHY WILSON	**129**

Disclaimer

Neither the publisher or the author is engaged in rendering professional advice or services to the individual reader. The ideas, procedures, and suggestions contained in this book are not intended as a substitute for consulting with your physician or mental health clinician. All matters regarding your health require medical supervision. Neither the author nor the publisher shall be liable or responsible for any loss or damage allegedly arising from any information or suggestion in this book.

Introduction

> "Decent people are so easy to manipulate."
> —Alastair "Mad-Eye" Moody, *Harry Potter and the Goblet of Fire*

I wrote the rough outline of this book in the form of an article for my website several years ago. That short piece of writing is still on my website, and I wrote it with the hope of reaching family and friends of people who had been the victim of a scam or fraud and giving them tools to help their loved one.

As time went on, I began to receive calls from all over the United States and sometimes from other countries as well, from people who had been scammed and sometimes from a family member or friend of someone who had been a victim. Some were looking for a counselor, some for information on resources that could help, and some simply needed to talk for a while to hear a kind word and feel a bit of hope again.

The level of shame that people feel in this situation is extreme, and sometimes feels almost tangible to me when I speak with them.

Many of those calls came in the middle of the night, from callers who did not want to give me their name.

It finally occurred to me that I needed to write this book to reach people who need that level of support but are far too embarrassed to reach out to others around them, a local therapist, or other support. Unfortunately, it is impossible for me to reach out to each person who reads this, but please know that this book itself is my best effort to figuratively reach out to help you find the resilience, courage, and healing you need.

It is impossible to know the true number of people who are and have been the victim of a scam. That shame and embarrassment prohibits far too many people from seeking help.

There were 4.7 million reports and 3.3 billion US dollars lost in scams or frauds in 2020, according to a February 2021 United States Federal Trade Commission report[1]. Those numbers represent *reported incidents only*. Imagine what those numbers would look like if we were able to measure the unreported crimes as well.

In addition to this disturbing information, there are not enough resources such as support groups to help individuals and their families to heal from the emotional impact of a scam or fraud.

People often feel very helpless and hopeless when they or someone they know has been scammed. Sadly, many are so overwhelmed, they attempt or complete suicide as a result. I hope that this book provides hope and healing for you, and enough for you to continue to reach out for support.

How to Use This Book

I've divided this book into three sections:

Part 1 - The Emotional Impact

Part 2 - How Did This Happen?

Part 3 - Healing and Recovery

I have added many headings in the table of contents for the purpose of allowing you to find the information you need the most.

My main goal in this book is to provide you with Part 3 so you can heal and regain a sense of empowerment in your life again. Parts 1 and 2 are important as well though.

Part 1 is included because I believe that understanding *all* of the potential emotional impact is important in that healing process, too. For many, shame, anger, and embarrassment are so strong it is difficult to see other emotional impacts as well. They are often there, though, and Part 1 can help you identify the ways you have been impacted emotionally to assist you in your own healing process.

All crime victims could benefit from identifying all of the impacts of the crime, for their own healing and also in preparing an impact statement that may be helpful for any court proceedings.

Part 2 offers some help in understanding how easily this can happen to *anyone*. The reasons for including this are:

- Right after fraud or a scam happens, the thoughts and emotions you probably have noticed the most are about disbelief, i.e. how could this possibly have happened? The thoughts "how could I be fooled so easily?" and "I should have known" echo in your mind again and again. This section can help you reduce or eliminate those thoughts.

- Another reason is to help you understand the tactics these criminals use. Scammers study human behavior; they carefully study concepts from psychology that put you at a disadvantage right away; and they do this in a systematic and devious way. *They do not care about you or the impact on you. They will use anything possible to get all they can from others.*

- The third reason is that scammers often share information about victims of scams and if you have been scammed once, you are more likely to be a target in the future. If that happens, you will be better prepared to recognize a scam and get out of that situation.

And finally, Part 3 offers a number of strategies you may use to find your own path to healing and recovery, as well as a chapter for guidance for family and friends, and another chapter for therapists.

It is possible that some examples and descriptions could be difficult for you to read, and you may have emotional reactions to them. It is fairly common for this to happen, so please:

- Be kind to yourself
- Take a break when needed
- Give yourself grace

Please note that throughout the book, I have chosen to use the word "scam" most often when describing what has happened, in the interest of making it as readable as possible. Each time I do, it represents all of the people who have been cheated, scammed, conned, defrauded, and all the other words that describe this terrible crime of having something taken from you through an act of persuasion and deception.

I tend to avoid using the word "victim." It can sometimes bring on the implication of being weak or that the person has given up, or even someone who is a pushover. I do not think this about you at all. It is the most commonly used word in our society, however, so I have chosen to use it up to this point.

From this point forward, when I can, I will use the word "survivor" instead. If you are reading this book, this word describes you more accurately. It implies strength, hope, courage, resilience, and perseverance. And, that is *you*.

One final thought about the way I've written this book. I've chosen to alternate using pronouns he, she, and they. My intention is to be inclusive, and also to keep the content as readable as possible.

Types of Scams

I have included some descriptions of different forms of scams in one of the Appendices of this book. However, detailing the different types of scams is not the main purpose of this book.

You'll notice that many examples of fraud or scam situations are provided throughout the book to show what I mean when I describe different ways a person may be affected by a scam, or when I describe how scammers use psychological principles against someone they target.

This is definitely not all the types of scams and fraud though. I have tended to use some relatively common scam situations, such as a romance scam, a consumer scam, identity theft, or impersonating a reputable company or an authority figure (such as law enforcement or the Internal Revenue Service in the United States government).

As you read, you will be thinking of the type of scam you experienced. Please keep in mind that some of the tactics used by scammers, or the emotional impact a person can experience, may not apply to every situation.

For those of you who have been scammed, it is my hope that in these pages, you will find healing, some relief from the pain you are feeling, and the courage to seek additional resources to support you.

Cathy Wilson, LPC, ACS

LifePaths Counseling Center
https://www.lifepathscounseling.com
Littleton, Colorado

Part 1 – The Emotional Impact of Being Scammed

Chapter 1: The Impact on Emotions and Thoughts

If you are the person who has been scammed, this chapter is not going to contain news for you. You already know there is a depth and intensity of emotions that can happen and has happened for you. My hope in describing this experience is that:

- You feel validated
- You feel heard
- You understand your own reactions better

For many people, the level of shock you likely have felt can leave you with so many emotions, it is difficult to understand the entire reaction, let alone to try and talk about it with someone (if you even can).

In the following pages, some of the emotional impacts are described. For some people, there is an internal judgement that you may have noticed, such as, "I should be over this by now," or, "I can't do anything to change the past, there's no reason to still be thinking about this." The impacts you'll find in this part of the book are the reasons you haven't "gotten over it" yet.

Shame

Shame is the grand-daddy of all the emotional impacts associated with being scammed. This is a powerful and difficult emotion. I don't think I can make an absolute statement that this happens to everyone who has been scammed, but it has to be close to every single person.

It is certainly a devastating way to feel and I know that I don't need to go in detail about what it feels like, or why you are feeling it. You'll find that it comes up multiple times through this book. Overcoming shame and its effects may be the most important part of your healing process and you will find more about overcoming shame in the chapter on healing.

Anger

Anger is also very powerful when it comes up in response to being scammed. You are likely to find yourself angry with the person you spoke with directly who scammed you, others helping this person, law enforcement in general for not doing something about this more effectively, the Internet, people who didn't figure out what was happening and stop it, and more. The person you are likely to be angry with the most, however, is *you*.

Grief and Loss

It may not have occurred to you that you are feeling grief after having been scammed or the survivor of fraud. Sometimes it can help in the healing process when you realize this is part of what you are feeling.

I mention both grief and loss in this section, so I can talk about both. Loss is a thing that happens – I can lose a person I care about, a job, or a home in a fire. Grief is our emotional response to the loss. Some potential losses for you may be obvious and some may not. Depending on the type of scam or fraud, here are some obvious ones:

- Money and financial security
- Love
- Time
- Possessions

The not-so-obvious ones, depending on the type of scam:

The Past and the Future - This type of loss is significant when it is a romance scam and you thought you were in an intimate relationship. There are outright promises about the future and some implied promises as well.

In addition, once you realize it has been a romance scam, the entire past of the relationship is changed. It isn't the budding romance you thought it was, it was a crime and you realize you've been violated in many ways. You have lost something very important to you.

Other types of scams result in future losses as well. Those with a significant financial loss may have impacted your retirement, or your future financial security in some way. It could have impacted what will be inherited from you, and so on.

This loss and the following one are very similar.

The Implied Promises in the "Relationship" (Romance Scam) - In a romance scam, there may have been promises that were openly discussed, such as those of commitment, loving, honoring, and cherishing each other. There were probably also implied promises of security, companionship, and support.

There is also the implied promise of a future you envisioned, whatever that looked like. *The relationship you thought you had is lost.*

In other scams, such as those related to jobs, the implied promise is that there is actually a job you are being considered for.

The Person You Thought They Were – Particularly in a romance scam, the person you thought you knew is now different. Sometimes, the way you see that person is *very* different. Memories of this person may come up for you, and the memory is changed now, too.

When you realize that you were interacting with a false self of that person, not their authentic self, it can be a shock and it can leave you feeling very angry, too.

If you didn't experience a romance scam, this loss may not be very significant at all for you.

And for some, the scam is relatively impersonal and there isn't a specific person associated with it. If so, you may not have noticed this type of loss at all.

The Person You Were - Your identity changes to some degree when you have been scammed. There is an entire chapter titled, The Impact on Identity (Chapter 3), however it is important to mention this here as a loss as well.

A very common sentiment I hear from people who have been scammed is, "I feel so stupid." How you see yourself has changed, which means the way you used to see yourself is now lost, and since this is a painful loss, you feel grief. My hope for you is that in reading this book, the way you see yourself begins to change for the better, and the grief eases.

Innocence - You might not immediately think of a loss of your own innocence when thinking about a scam or fraud you have had to deal with. It often is a loss, however. Realizing that there are people who will take advantage of you in this way and cause you harm represents a loss of innocence.

Hope – Depending on the type of scam or fraud, and what you have lost in the process, a loss of hope often happens, too. People have lost their life savings, or they have felt that they can't possibly trust again after a romance scam.

Self-Respect – Another common sentiment I hear are several types of statements that indicate a person has lost respect for themselves, such as, "I can't believe I let this happen."

Embarrassment

For many of us, it is difficult to distinguish between shame, embarrassment, and guilt. Or, it may be that they are so intertwined it doesn't matter much which is which. Embarrassment is important to mention because this is another emotion that will keep you isolated from others, and hiding what has happened. Isolating and hiding this keeps you from receiving much needed support, though.

You may be anticipating being judged by others. Let's be realistic, some people do judge, and if others in your life know or find out about the scam it is possible that you'll hear judgment in their response. It may help to think about this: I have noticed that sometimes people judge others out of a subconscious need to feel superior, and have a false sense of control as if the same hardship can't happen to them.

Guilt

Guilt may come up for you if being a survivor of a scam has impacted people in your life that you care about. If you lost a great deal of money to someone, your children or your partner would inherit less. If you put your last dollars into a scam that you thought was going to be a new job, the hardship on your family may be greater now than it was before.

Anxiety and Fear

It is very natural to feel anxious and fearful after being scammed. Particularly if you consider this a traumatic experience. Many people do consider a scam or fraud to be traumatic. Trauma is not limited to events that cause a loss of life or serious injury. It can come from anything you experience that felt threatening or very disturbing.

Depending on the type of scam, there may be some level of trauma for you. Over time, this will ease, but for now, understanding that this is an expected response to having been threatened may help you stop feeling even more shame.

You may also notice feeling more general anxiety and fear all the time, or when you must interact with strangers, or when you are worried that someone may find out what happened to you.

Depression

As the realization sinks in that you have been scammed or the survivor of fraud, many people experience a deep depression as a result. Your sleep may be disturbed, as well as your eating habits. You may have little to no energy, or motivation, or sense of pleasure in life. This also will ease over time, particularly if you actively work on your own healing process.

Far too many people have thoughts of suicide, or may even act on these thoughts. If you are having thoughts like this, please reach out to a supportive person in your life or a professional in mental health for help. In the United States (US), you can also call the National Suicide Hotline at any time and speak to someone in English or Spanish, at 1-800-273-8255.

You can also seek out other types of emergency services in your area, such as by calling 911 in the US or a similar service in other countries; or by going to a local emergency hospital.

You can choose not to tell anyone about the reason why you are having these thoughts, and still get help for yourself.

Please try to remember that you won't always feel this way. Many people recall past difficult situations that they were able to overcome, as a way to support the idea that they will overcome this situation as well.

Disbelief and Shock

It is common to have a hard time believing that this has happened to you, and to feel shock as the full realization comes over you. You may review many details, the timeline of how things happened, and "evidence," when you are in this state, hoping that you are wrong.

It is a very natural response to keep thinking about those details and try to make sense of something that feels unbelievable.

Damaged Self-Worth

I included this here because there is a great deal of emotion in this concept, however, Chapter 3 – The Impact on Identity goes into more detail on how self-worth can be damaged when a person has been scammed. It is common to have difficulty trusting yourself and feel self-doubt in many ways.

For some, there is an element of "societal condemnation[2]" that comes up. An example of this is if you yourself have ever thought or said that if someone is stupid enough to fall for a scam, they deserve what they get, that concept could be bothering you a lot right now. You may still believe it, and be scolding and blaming yourself. This belief is not helpful, and it also isn't true. No one deserves to have this happen. And, the fault lies with the criminals behind it, not you.

You may also feel that you somehow deserved this, or "had it coming" for something you have done in the past. This could be because of something specific, or just a general sense that you "must have" done something to deserve it. You did not. Scammers are ruthless criminals, and this happened because they do not care how their actions affect others.

What Can You Do to Feel Better?

Things you can do to help yourself through the healing and recovery process after being scammed is covered in other chapters in this book, but I am also including a few ideas below:

Accept the emotions – Those are some ugly feelings in the list above. When a person has been scammed, they will often suffer for a long time. It is normal to feel these emotions, and at the same time, they shouldn't last forever. It may be that you are fighting these feelings and trying to avoid them in any way possible. Believe me, I understand wanting to do this. However, it isn't likely you will escape them. Sometimes emotions simply must be felt and expressed before they start to ease up. If you can find a way to safely let the emotions happen, accept that they are there, it is very possible that they will lose some of the power they have over you and will lose their intensity.

Find your best supportive family members and friends – If you can, tell someone you trust and who is emotionally safe for you. Being embarrassed and worrying about being judged were mentioned above. Think about the people in your life and seek out those that are least likely to judge you and add to the shame you already feel.

Self-care – Find ways to care for yourself the best you can. There is an entire chapter in this book on self-care and hopefully one of the ideas in that section will be something that appeals to you and eases the burden you are carrying right now.

Ask for help – You may be telling yourself that you "should" be able to handle this, you "should" be fine, or that you are making more out of this than you "should." Stop. This is hard. It is okay if you are struggling. Consider some ways you can ask for help from a friend or family member, or ask for help with a therapist.

Chapter 2: The Impact on Relationships

Along with the impact on emotion, you have probably noticed that your relationships are suffering to some degree as well. Humans need relationships, though, and understanding how this could be impacted and what you can do about it will also be essential to your healing process.

You need other people around you, *your people*, to help you heal.

Loss of Trust in Others

All forms of scams and fraud are also a betrayal. Even if it was a small level, you trusted a person who scammed or cheated you in some way, your trust was broken, and now you are trying to get past feeling betrayed.

It will take a while before you trust others again. When a scam or fraud is still recent, many situations and people in your life are seen through a new and skeptical lens, with you feeling something like this: "If that person could fool me and I completely believed them, how do I know you aren't trying to fool me, too?"

What happened has also damaged your ability to trust yourself, too. You may have a lot of self-doubt and question your thoughts, your intuition, or your judgement of situations or people.

Your Partner Feels Betrayed

You may be arguing with your partner who also feels betrayed after being scammed. If your partner is affected by a loss of money/financial security, or if you were involved with a romance scam, and you were also emotionally, physically, financially, or spiritually unfaithful to the relationship, your partner is likely dealing with many of the same emotions you are; plus, your partner is also feeling betrayed by you.

Others close to you may feel betrayed as well, if there is a financial loss that results in less inheritance, less security, or a change in lifestyle.

Taking Your Emotions Out on Others

You may also have difficulty in your closest relationships because your emotions are so intense that you are taking them out on people you care about.

Many of us are not aware of it at first when we take our emotions out on others. If you aren't sure, you may choose to ask one of your family members or friends if you are doing this. You could also choose to be more observant and notice others' reactions to you and the things you say.

A lot of people will tolerate this for a while because they care about you, but if you let it go on too long your loved ones may mention it or remind you that they are on your side!

Isolation and Withdrawing

The shame, embarrassment, guilt, and other difficult emotions may make you want to avoid people you care about. You may feel judged, even if no one is judging you.

If you do this, however, you are losing quality time with the people important to you, and you need that connection in your healing.

Ruminating and Not Getting "Over It"

Ruminating, or talking again and again about what has happened and how you are feeling can leave others with less and less patience to listen and support you.

This is actually a natural thing that we do, however. A few of the things our brains are designed to do are to solve problems, or to figure out situations to keep us safe and away from hurt. When you have been scammed, you ruminate about it as your brain naturally attempts to find what went wrong, or to find something you could have done differently. It's looking for the moment when you "should have known," even though that may not be possible.

You want to find a solution, but you can't "fix" what has already happened. Your brain is still working subconsciously on the problem, though, and trying to do exactly that. I am not in any way saying to you, "Just get over it already." That statement is dismissing of all you are experiencing.

What I am saying is be aware of this happening so you can more consciously choose when you are thinking and talking about what happened, and also choose how you are thinking about it. In the process of being more aware of when you begin to ruminate, an extra benefit is that you will also be aware of the impact on those around you and preserve that support you need from them the best you can.

Changed View of Relationships

Depending on the type of scam and how much you have been impacted, you may experience a significant change in how you see relationships. This experience could mean that your willingness to be emotionally intimate with another person has changed. Relationships may seem risky now, and as a result, no longer worth it.

Separating the Fictitious Person from the Criminal

This is a difficult process, particularly for those who experienced a romance scam. At first, it is very difficult to separate the person you thought they were, from the person you now know to be a criminal. At the same time, this process is necessary and involves grieving for the person you thought they were, and acceptance of the situation as it is.

What Can You Do to Feel Better?

Ask for help – As in the previous chapter, ask for help when you are having a hard time. This is a very difficult situation to recover from. With many people, you can strengthen relationships and restore connection when you ask for their help.

Own up to it – If you read this and realized that you have been doing one or more of the things listed above that can negatively impact relationships (such as taking your emotions out on others), tell those people you realized it. Talk about it and then follow this up with the effort to stop the behaviors that are creating barriers to connecting with people who are important to you.

Consciously connect with others – After reading this chapter, you may have realized some things that are affecting the important relationships in your life. It may help you to consciously make an effort to connect with one or more people you care about, and talk through anything that has impacted these relationships. This can help you repair any ruptures that may have occurred.

Dr. Brené Brown is a researcher who has studied shame and how it can be a barrier to connection with others. You may be interested to explore some of her videos or books, such as *Dare to Lead*[3], to help you strengthen your connection with others. In particular, her BRAVING model described in this book is an excellent guide when deciding who to trust and connect with. BRAVING is a way to remember that the people to trust have these qualities: Boundaries, Reliability, Accountability, Vault (they keep confidences), Integrity, Nonjudgment, and Generosity.

Self-care – As in the previous chapter, self-care is important in healing and maintaining your mental health. Please take a look at Chapter 9 – Self-Care to find ideas to help care for yourself.

Chapter 3: The Impact on Identity

You may not have thought about the impact on your identity until reading this book. There is a great deal of change to identity that happens for people, however, when a scam or fraud has happened.

The main thing I have noticed is the difficulty in having to come to terms with the fact that you are now a person who was fooled by another, and for many, there were big consequences to that.

Here are some more specific changes in identity that individuals may struggle with:

Lack of Trust in Yourself and Self-Doubt

Chances are very good that since you were scammed, you don't trust yourself anymore. How can you trust your own judgment and perception after someone fooled you so completely? It may seem impossible to get this back, but it is not. Part of what is included in this book are the ways we get fooled by other people and situations (Part 2). It is included to help you learn more about what has happened, know how to combat those things, and eventually be able to trust yourself again.

Lack of Security in the World

After a traumatic experience or a betrayal, a person will naturally feel less safe and secure in the world. You read about the loss of innocence in Chapter 1, and now you have felt first-hand how there are dangerous and vile people who really will take whatever they can from you, with no apparent remorse.

As with lack of trust, my hope is that the more you understand about how people can be tricked, your sense of security in the world will come back to you as well. It may have a more realistic and cautious side to it, but it typically comes back.

Beliefs about Self, Others, and the World

From very early in development, each human being is developing beliefs about their own self, about other people, and about the world. This continues throughout life and most changes are subtle and we aren't aware of them. A significant event in our life can have a very obvious and conscious effect, however, such as being scammed.

For instance, before this happened, you may have felt strongly that people are inherently "good," or that there is "more 'good' in the world than 'bad.'" You may not feel that way anymore and feel that the entire world has changed for you.

You Are Not Stupid

After speaking with hundreds of people who have been scammed, a belief that has a huge impact on people is that they now see themselves as stupid. I have heard this word and many others that mean the same thing, and phrases expressing this same sentiment. It seems that each person struggles with the conclusion that they must not be intelligent since this could happen, and the internal conflict of never having seen themselves this way before.

You aren't stupid. *You made a mistake*. Humans can make mistakes without having to see themselves as stupid.

What Can You Do to Feel Better?

Change the narrative – Each of us has a certain way of telling ourselves our own life story or narrative, and this changes through life as we learn, experience, and understand more. If you picked up this book, I suspect that the narrative going on for you has taken a very negative turn. Look for ways to change this narrative to include more about the strengths you have developed as a result of what happened, such as your resilience, and your ability to recover.

Monitor your thinking – Watch for thoughts that reveal how you are now seeing yourself. As you become aware of these, if there are shaming or unhelpful thoughts, is there a way to challenge those thoughts and change them to healthier and more helpful ways of thinking about yourself?

Self-Care – Are you wondering if I am going to keep bringing up self-care through this book? Yes, I *am*. You need "down time" when you aren't worrying about what has happened, time to engage in an activity you enjoy, and all that comes with self-care. Please find a way to incorporate this into your life, particularly now.

Part 2 – How Did This Happen?

Chapter 4: Humans are Not Perfect

This chapter, along with chapters 5-8 here in Part 2, are written to help you see how easy it is to trick a person, just with a little knowledge about psychology, the brain and human behavior.

People are not perfect, and this shows up in so many ways! It may show up by making mistakes, saying things we don't really mean, acting selfishly at times, or getting our priorities mixed up. When it comes to getting scammed, the human imperfection we are focused on is making mistakes in the form of errors in thinking.

It is likely that you have concluded that you must be a lot less intelligent than you thought you were. Many people come to this conclusion after being scammed.

If we look at being scammed realistically, there are other aspects of the situation that outweigh any level of intelligence. As you read this part of the book, I hope you keep in your mind that people who scam others have studied these concepts thoroughly, and practiced them, and they have no hesitation in harming you and others[4]. *They are very good at it.* I can't emphasize this fact enough. The average person is no match for someone that is not only *skilled* at harming other people, they are *willing* to harm other people. You aren't either of those.

Another factor to keep in mind is that scammers will use these tactics along with your own vulnerability, pain, need, or fear. The lonelier a person is, the more likely that person will be influenced by the skills of a romance scammer. The more pain you want to avoid with the IRS, the more you will be influenced by the tactics of an IRS scammer.

Scammers also often look and sound like average, common people. You can probably come up with a few stereotypes that fit the "image" of a shady character. If a scammer looked like one of these stereotypes we have picked up from television and movies, we wouldn't be fooled. They look like average, common people on purpose to keep us from being on guard.

Many people tend to be trusting in nature and we rely on visual cues and our experiences in life to decide whether to trust someone – if a person looks trusting from our past experiences, it is less likely you will be alerted to any danger.

Finally, there are countless ways that tactics from all four of the following can be combined, and as a result, can deceive very smart people. This is sometimes referred to as "social engineering" or using human psychological and sociological principles to deceive and influence others.

Manipulation – In Chapter 5, I have separated forms of manipulation into two kinds: one of these is manipulation based in deception and the other is manipulation based in control. You have been lied to, which meant you based your decision or decisions on false information. It is also likely that some manipulation was meant to be controlling or to coerce you into making the decision or decisions you did.

Psychological Biases – There are many forms of psychological bias that affect how we think about situations. Psychological biases are sometimes intentional and we are aware of them, but we are going to focus in this book on the biases that are unintentional and out of our awareness.

For instance, one that may be influencing you right now as you are reading this book is called the Hindsight Bias. It means that we have a tendency to think that when we made a decision in the past, we had the same knowledge that we do today. When you have said to yourself, "I should have known," when berating yourself about falling for a scam, you are unintentionally believing that your past self would have had all the information to make a different decision. You didn't, though. Some examples of psychological biases are details in Chapter 6.

Cognitive or Thought Distortions – Cognitive distortions are forms of thinking that are not logical, and often can cause a person distress. For instance, "all-or-nothing thinking" means that a person tends to see all or nothing in situations or people. It is sometimes seen as minimizing or maximizing situations as well, by saying things like "You always do that," or, "I never get my way." You can see how the words "always" and "never" can increase a person's level of emotion and also are unlikely to be true.

Thinking to yourself that you are "so stupid" could be thought of as all-or-nothing thinking. Applying this label to your entire self is not accurate; thinking, "I made a mistake," is realistic, accurate, and much less distressing.

Cognitive distortions are detailed in Chapter 7.

Persuasion Techniques – These are techniques that may be used in a variety of settings to influence another person. Some are well-known advertising strategies. You'll find these in Chapter 8.

Use the information in these upcoming chapters to understand how these techniques are used and how you were taken advantage of, so you can be more aware and cautious in the future. You can't change the past, but you can build your own critical thinking skills, prepare yourself, and prevent a similar thing from happening again.

Chapter 5: Forms of Manipulation

There are many forms of manipulation. This chapter contains two lists to describe these: Manipulation in the form of deception, and manipulation in the form of control. You will see some overlap in these lists. Sometimes it is useful to list a type of manipulation in multiple ways.

The information in this chapter is included because, when you gain understanding about manipulation, you will often find methods that you hadn't thought of before. This helps you to be more aware of when someone is trying to manipulate you.

The hope is that you will now be more likely to recognize it and name it in that moment. Do you recall a time when you felt pretty sure you were being manipulated by someone, but you couldn't come up with words to describe what was happening? *When you can name it in that moment*, it helps you to describe what is happening. You then have a better chance of resisting the influence, and finding a better way to respond than you might have in the past.

Although many forms of manipulation on this list may not apply to the type of scam or fraud you experienced, I have included them all. This list (with a few modifications) was originally published in a book I wrote about dealing with toxic relationships, titled *Boundaries of Steel: A Workbook for Managing and Recovering from Toxic Relationships*[5].

It is likely that you will also notice that some of these have been used in other situations in your life.

Manipulation in the Form of Deception

Gaslighting – This is the superstar of all forms of manipulation. It is also sometimes referred to as "crazy-making." Gaslighting is happening when a person lies about or questions your perception of others, yourself, or situations until you begin to question your perception yourself. You begin to doubt that you have good judgment, and start to wonder if you are crazy or losing your mind.

The term comes from a 1944 movie titled *Gaslight*[6] in which a husband gradually attempts to make his wife believe she is insane. One of the manipulative tactics he used was to dim the gaslights in their home, while claiming that it didn't happen and she was imagining it.

Lying, Partial Truths, and Lies of Omission – Misleading someone by withholding the truth is often a first step in manipulation, followed by other forms of manipulation in order to avoid the consequences of having lied.

Denial – This is a rejection of the truth, sometimes even when presented with solid evidence.

Spin – Creating a biased or skewed interpretation that is designed to be favorable towards this person.

Deflection or Diversion – The use of some means to get the attention off of what you are discussing (by distraction, turning it back on you, changing the subject, blaming others).

Projection – Projecting what is going on with that person, onto you. If they are lying, they accuse you of lying; if they are acting out in anger, they accuse you of doing that, etc.

Faking Empathy or Remorse – The person may appear to express with body language and/or words that they feel empathy or remorse, or they may say that they are sorry, but the unhealthy behavior continues.

Claims Misunderstanding – Although you feel sure that the person understood what you meant or wanted, they claim not to after failing to meet your needs, meet a commitment, etc. (gaslighting might take this form).

Love Bombing – A way to idealize you with excessive expressions of love or desire; and sometimes there is a cycle of love bombing, then devaluing you, then discarding you. This is a "red flag." It often shows up as repeated adoring statements, texts, and emojis that feel "over the top" or too early for your current relationship stage.

Sarcasm or Humor – The person may use these to distract you from the original subject of conversation, or to deflect. It may come out as "I was just joking around," or a similar statement.

Focusing on How You Communicate, Not the Message – This is when the person stays focused on how you deliver a message, rather than addressing the message itself. This is a form of deflection but worth noting because it is relatively common. For instance, the person might say, "Our therapist said we need to use 'I statements 'and you aren't doing that."

Bait and Switch – This is when the person offers or promises something fun or rewarding, but the reality is that it turns out to be unpleasant to some degree, often to a high degree! Empty promises can fit in this category.

"Backhanded" compliments – Although the person may be phrasing a statement as a compliment and at first it appears that way, there is an underlying message that can also be interpreted as an insult. An example would be a statement such as, "Wow, I didn't expect you to do that well on your presentation."

Passive-aggressive behavior – This may take the form of "forgetting" or procrastinating doing something the person agreed to do but doesn't really want to.

"Blaming the survivor" or blaming others – A person who doesn't want to accept responsibility for something they have done may use this behavior to avoid responsibility. For instance, saying, "I wouldn't have had to ask you for so much money if you had responded sooner," is blaming you for their problem.

The acronym "DARVO" has been used to describe this behavior and it stands for "Deny, Attack, and Reverse Victim and Offender.[7]" It was initially used to describe how a sex offender may avoid responsibility for their behavior and it applies in many similar interactions. The person who behaved in an offensive way will deny that they did anything wrong, attack the accuser, and then attempt to make the victim/survivor out to be the offender.

They are "tofu" – Sometimes a person will act as if they agree with everything another person says or does, essentially taking on the "flavor" of whoever they are with, in order to get people to like them or do what they want. *When someone seems similar to you, it is easier to trust and feel safe with them.*

"I'm sorry, but…" - This is likely to be a non-apology. The person says the words of an apology in their statement somewhere, but then it turns out to be a false apology. Any apology that starts with "I'm sorry, but…" is potentially questionable. Often, what follows is some reason why they are not accountable for what the person did. "I'm sorry you feel that way" and "I'm sorry you see it that way" are also often a form of non-apologies.

Manipulation in the Form of Control

Accusation That You Are Controlling – This is also a form of deflection or gaslighting, but worth noting because often when people first start to set boundaries with another person, they are accused of being "controlling." It isn't being controlling if you are focused on what you need, and attempting to take care of yourself.

If you are focused on trying to get this person to change, and this is a subtle difference, then you are trying to control that person. A very important part of this is your intention and the emotion that goes with it.

These same words that are delivered kindly and firmly can be a boundary, while when delivered with anger, sarcasm, or resentment are controlling: "I really don't like being late, and I also don't like feeling like a nag about it. So, to solve this situation, the next time we are supposed to be somewhere and it is important to me to be on time, I'll take my car and meet you there instead of driving together."

Minimizing – Trying to convince you that the subject in question is not as important as it really is.

Extreme and Shifting Emotions – This is the use of displaying emotion in a way that is intended to shift the focus, gain sympathy, get you to back down, etc. It could be crying/sobbing, acting out in anger, silent pouting, or other emotional displays;

and often will switch between them if a particular emotion doesn't seem to be working.

Punishment – The person may use emotional, financial, physical, or other means to "punish" you for something they didn't like, for setting a boundary, making a mistake, etc. For instance, it could be "the silent treatment," or they may withhold sex or affection.

Guilt-Tripping – Fostering a sense of guilt in you, to get you to agree to what the person wants as if you are obligated to do certain things.

Playing the Survivor – Either beating themselves up excessively, or making statements to foster sympathy from you, such as "I guess I can't do anything right."

Double Standards – The person has different standards for you and for themselves, such as it is okay for them to be unavailable without explanation, but you cannot.

Going to Extremes – Using language that gets emotions running higher or exaggerating circumstances. For instance, saying, "I am the worst person ever" or "You are the worst person ever."

Using Triggers/Pushing Buttons – The person consciously or subconsciously makes statements or behaves in a way that is a trigger or emotional button for you; the payoff for your partner is that this will often derail the conversation and they can avoid taking responsibility for their own actions, or it gives them a reason to redirect attention to your reaction rather than the core issue being discussed.

Attention-Seeking Behavior – This can be either positive or negative behavior, but it is intended to get some kind of reaction from others – validation, sympathy, anger, etc.

Wearing You Down – When someone relentlessly keeps talking, following you around the house, calling or repeatedly bringing up what they want, it may be easier to give in than to keep enduring the constant pressure. This is also harassment.

Isolating – This is a way of gaining more control and power over you by gradually getting you to withdraw from other support systems such as friends, family, or activities or communities you enjoy. It may take the form of moving you farther from these support systems (moving to a new place you live). It can also be gradually becoming more and more negative about your family or friends, encouraging you to withdraw from those relationships. Another form this could take is repeated comments about how much time an activity or group takes away from the relationship until you give in and stop doing it.

Using children or pets – Sadly, children and pets are too often a tool or a pawn for a manipulator. There are too many ways to list here in how they are used. One very common one is using the children as a shield to avoid being confronted about unhealthy behaviors ("we can't talk about this now, the kids are in the next room."). A manipulative person may also use pets by not letting you see a loved pet, or threatening harm.

In a romance scam, the scammer may claim to have children or pets that are affected by fictitious terrible circumstances, to gain your sympathy and gain an advantage in getting you to send money.

Using others ("flying monkeys") – This is a form of triangulation, or using others to manipulate a person. Triangulation is getting someone else involved in a conflict you have between you, in an effort to get you to change or stop holding a boundary. This can take many forms, and one of them is often referred to as "flying monkeys," where a person talks badly about you to others. It can result in getting others to reject you, confront you, or talk bad about you to others with the hope that you will feel punished or change your boundaries.

An example of this may be a neighbor you have a conflict with. If the neighbor speaks badly about you to other neighbors, giving only enough detail to sway the others to their "side," it can lead to those other neighbors being allies with the manipulator, rejecting you and possibly continuing the negative talk about you to others. This can ultimately lead you to feel isolated and unwelcome in your own neighborhood.

In a scam, employing the use of others with authority will often give their situation the appearance of credibility. If they claim to be in the hospital and need your help with medical bills, they may have someone pose as a doctor to add this credibility.

Using spirituality – Manipulators will often use your own values or beliefs against you, and using religion or spirituality is very common.

Sleep deprivation – This is a form of emotional and even physical abuse. Although it may be a person's subconscious effort at controlling another, it can also be a very purposeful effort as well. Either way, it will wear you down, reduce your cognitive abilities, and increase your emotional vulnerability.

For instance, in a romance scam, the scammer may want you to agree to something that you are uncomfortable with, such as sending a nude photo of yourself. If you refuse to agree, they may bring this up at a time when you need to sleep, become relentless about this, in the hopes that you will need to sleep so badly you will agree even though you don't want to.

Creating fear or false urgency – If the manipulative person can promote fear or a sense of urgency in you, it may convince you to go along with what they want from you.

"No win" situation – This is also referred to as a double bind, or "damned if you do, damned if you don't." For instance, in a romance scam, if you realize what has happened and say you are going to report the person to law enforcement, if the scammer then reveals that they have compromising video or photos of you and will expose this if you report them, they have created a no-win situation.

Name-calling, yelling, cursing – A manipulative person may use these behaviors as a tool to coerce you to do what they want. If this is a consistent response, you may tend to avoid ever upsetting them if possible, to avoid experiencing the pain of their reaction.

Undermining your values– This often shows up as a consistent and systematic way to weaken your resolve in a particular situation or devalue you.

Undermining your important relationships – This also is likely to be a consistent and systematic way of devaluing you. It isolates you, and weakens you by removing potentially supportive people in your life. In doing so, this can make you more dependent on the scammer to have your emotional needs met.

Taking advantage of a time when you are vulnerable – This could happen if someone waits until the last minute and does a poor job on something so that you have to rush to complete it; or it could take the form of a romance scam intended to take advantage of someone who is extremely lonely.

Telling you your needs are "weakness" – When a person doesn't want to put in the effort to meet your needs in some way, they may frame your request as a weakness to get you to stop asking for those needs to be met.

Demanding an explanation - When someone does this and you do offer an explanation, the response is often to undermine it, challenge it, or tell you that you are wrong. The purpose is to get you to withdraw the boundary or what you are requesting of that person.

Subtle or hidden meanings - A form of manipulation often used in abusive relationships is to make statements that have a hidden meaning between the two of you. Once the hidden meaning is established, the abusive partner can use that word or phrase no matter who is around as an effort to feel in control.

Chapter 6: Psychological Biases

On the following pages, you will find examples of psychological biases. Becoming familiar with these can help you become aware of when they are happening in your thoughts, which then gives you the ability to overcome them.

As mentioned at the end of Chapter 4 – Humans are Not Perfect, psychological biases are sometimes intentional and we are aware of them, but we are going to focus in this book on the biases that are unintentional and out of our awareness.

This isn't a complete list. I have chosen to highlight the biases that seem to apply best in situations when a person is trying to persuade you in some way.

Not all of these would have had an effect on your thinking at the time you were scammed. When you think about the examples, however, they illustrate how easy it is to be influenced and not be aware of the power of a bias.

Negativity Bias - People tend towards believing negative things far more easily than positive things. You have to work at it to give both positives and negatives equal consideration. Many scams use fear of negative consequences to persuade you, such as in a false claim that there is a warrant for your arrest or the IRS scam that claims you owe taxes.

Confirmation Bias - People tend to pay more attention to things that confirm our opinion; we more easily see evidence that confirms our thoughts as opposed to evidence that would challenge our thoughts. When a scam involves something that you want, a confirmation bias could cause you to stop looking any further. It makes you tend to believe what you want to believe or what you agree with, and if it causes you to stop checking all facts, you may fall for a scam.

Hindsight Bias - We hold our past selves accountable for things we know today, as if we also knew it at some point in the past. In the present, you see red flags or clues that happened, and it sheds new light on events of the past. You will have to work at it to avoid thinking that you "should have known" back then what you know today.

False Consensus - We tend to think that people agree with our opinion, or that "most people" do this or that, believe this or that, etc. If a scammer sets up something that appears to indicate that a lot of people have already, for instance, invested in what they are trying to persuade you to invest in, it could be enough for you to decide to go ahead and join in. For instance, scammers may create hundreds of false social media accounts to make it appear that "many people" are making a lot of money in the "investment" they have proposed to you.

Control Fallacy - We either tend to think that we have more control than we actually do, or less control than we actually do. This acts as a defense mechanism, in the way that we need it to. It takes mental work to accurately perceive how much control we have in a particular situation.

Being judgmental of others is a good example of this. If I were to believe that an intelligent person won't be fooled by a scammer, I can falsely assure myself that since I am intelligent, it cannot happen to me. This can give me a false sense of having more control than I actually do, particularly when I don't take biases, cognitive distortions, and forms of manipulation under consideration. It also blames the survivor.

After a scam, a person may convince themselves there was "nothing" they could have done, in order to cope with how devastating it has been to be scammed. This is a false sense of no control.

The actual truth is somewhere in the middle, isn't it? A person can educate themselves on the ways a scammer can deceive you and prepare themselves in the best possible way; and at the same time acknowledge that scammers will go to great lengths to persuade others and it is possible that in certain circumstances, any of us may be misled.

Implicit Bias - Our brain is designed to categorize things to help save mental energy and work most efficiently; but this works against us to create an implicit bias. This bias is what causes a person to stereotype another or categorize that other person. People often act on this bias subconsciously. This can affect how you perceive certain behaviors in others.

It also means that we tend to trust other people who look and act like we do. Scammers will often know enough about you to use a person that has characteristics that are similar to yours, or characteristics that are similar to people associated with you. Or they may simply use a type of person that others tend to trust more than otherwise, such as an older woman or a woman with children.

For instance, now that you are educating yourself on scammer behaviors, and this has happened to you, you may notice that your implicit bias is to see every person trying to sell you something as being a scammer. Not everyone you meet is trying to manipulate you but it can sure seem that way after a scam.

Dunning-Kruger Effect - This bias refers to when a person with relatively limited knowledge or ability in a certain area may personally believe that they have more knowledge or ability than they actually do. Sometimes a person may believe they have more than another who actually *does* have extensive knowledge or ability on a subject.

If I see myself as relatively intelligent, this may lead me to believe that I am better at recognizing a scam than I actually am.

Self-Serving Bias - The tendency to take credit for positive things, but blame something external for negative things. For instance, a parent might find it much easier to take credit for a child's accomplishments but not the child's shortcomings.

A scammer may create a feeling of alliance with you by congratulating you on a positive aspect of the situation, or blaming something external when an aspect is negative, to gain your favor or goodwill.

Sunk Cost Fallacy - A person's tendency to stay with something longer because of the time already invested (like a relationship), even when all signs indicate it is time to stop (i.e., end the relationship). If there is an element of gambling to a scam, the tendency to stay with it just a little longer to recoup what you've lost can be very strong.

Optimism Bias - A person's tendency to believe that they are less likely to experience a negative event. For instance, an adolescent's tendency to feel invincible. Or, the tendency to feel that this can't possibly be a romance scam because you have thoughts such as "I can tell this person really loves me," or "Our relationship is different."

Pessimism Bias - Naturally, this is the opposite of the Optimism Bias above. A person may have a tendency to believe that bad things are always going to happen to them, or that future events will have a negative outcome. A scammer may use this to their advantage to persuade you to do something to avoid a negative outcome.

Chapter 7: Cognitive Distortions

Cognitive distortions or thought distortions are very common ways of thinking, and sometimes natural ways the brain is designed to process information. Like with psychological biases, it takes work to overcome these ways of thinking, but with practice you can more often catch yourself when you are doing it.

The benefit of understanding these is to understand how these could have been used to influence you. Remember, scammers study the ways people tend to think very carefully. This knowledge of human tendencies is what makes them successful in their scam. *They are very good at this.*

A scammer may utilize these concepts in the way information is presented to you, in order to exploit these tendencies.

Or, you could be under the influence of some of these ways of thinking now, after the scam.

You'll find some crossover in this list, and I have allowed for that because there are times when hearing a concept in one way doesn't resonate, while it will make sense when described in another way. Also, as with the list of psychological biases in the previous chapter, this is not a complete list of every form of cognitive distortion.

Filtering - Magnifying the negative aspects of a situation while filtering out all the positives.

All-or-nothing thinking - Everything is polarized such as being all bad, always late, never enough. There are no gray areas.

Overgeneralization - Coming to a general conclusion after one event or incident; you expect the same outcome for all experiences after having one experience. For instance, now that a scam has happened to you, you may have so little trust in yourself that you won't go anywhere or do anything alone. You are afraid that anything you do will lead to another scam.

Jumping to Conclusions - We create a story about something happening without having proof – a scammer can present information in a way that makes it appear that this scam is the "only way" to avoid a negative outcome.

Catastrophizing - You expect things to go bad, no matter what.

Minimizing or Maximizing – A tendency to think in terms of one extreme or the other.

Personalization - It's about me, no matter what, and I don't look for proof or evidence that the reality may be about something else.

Control Fallacy - The belief that I can control things I really can't. Some examples are believing superstitions, or that you are responsible for everyone having a good time at a party.

Fairness Fallacy - A person gets resentful because they "know" what is fair but no one agrees with them, or that person believes that life "should" be fair.

Blaming - The act of holding other people responsible for your own pain, reaction, emotion, or thought. In reality, no one can make another person feel or think anything.

Shoulds - The emotional consequence is guilt if you are directing "should" statements towards yourself, and people often respond with anger if it comes from someone else. "Shoulds" feel punishing. Replacing this word with "could" or "I could choose to" is more accurate.

Emotional Reasoning - Believing that "if I feel that way, it must be true" and applying your feelings about a situation or subject to others.

Change Fallacy - The belief that other people will change if I want them to, or that I have the power to convince them to change.

Global Labelling - The belief that "everyone feels this way" or "no one feels that way." Or, one seemingly bad behavior in a person and you conclude they are a "bad person."

Always being right - Everyone around a person is on trial to show that their opinion or thoughts are absolutely correct, and they must justify it.

Heaven's reward fallacy - If a person does everything right, sacrifices a lot, serve others, etc., they will eventually get what they want or deserve.

Chapter 8: Persuasion Techniques

Persuasion techniques are used in many common circumstances, such as sales or advertising. Informal interactions between people can often have an element of persuasion, too, such as between friends, within families, at the workplace, and more.

Although the idea of persuasion has a more negative association, situations between people that involve persuasion may not necessarily be negative. For instance, if you are afraid to have a surgery you need, your partner and your doctor may utilize some forms of persuasion to help you see a more complete view of the situation and persuade you to go ahead with the surgery.

However, persuasion techniques is another skill area that scammers study and get very good at, in order to influence you. They are used in combination with various manipulation tactics, psychological biases, and cognitive biases you read about in the previous chapters.

As with the previous two chapters, this is not a complete list of all forms of persuasion. These are tactics that are commonly used in scams.

Authority – The use of a person in authority gives a situation credibility, and an authority figure gets our attention quickly. Scams that appear to be from a person with the IRS or someone in law enforcement are good examples of the use of authority as a method of persuasion.

Get a "Yes" Early On – If a person is trying to persuade you and can get you to start "saying yes" to questions or agreeing in response to what is being presented to you, you are more likely to continue feeling and acting agreeable as the stakes get higher.

Bait and Switch – This is when someone presents a product or service with certain qualities and price, but then switches it to something less valuable for the price you pay. If you order a product online that appears to be a quantity of four, but you are only shipped a quantity of one, that was a bait and switch.

Knowing a Secret – If we feel like we are one of only a few who can know a secret, we are drawn to purchasing a product or service that offers this.

Commitment or Consistency – Once a person is out in the open about something they like or an affiliation, they are more likely to stay with it. This could be a product, place of business, or viewpoint.

Reciprocity – If you receive something, you are more inclined to give something back.

Urgency – Creating a sense of urgency translates into a potential loss, and can compel a person to make a purchase or go along with what someone wants to avoid losing something they see as valuable.

Scarcity – The more we believe that something is rare or a limited supply, psychologically, the more we want it.

Social Proof – The more it appears that many people do what is being asked of you or buy a certain product or service, the more likely you are to also do that.

Liking – The more we like a person, the more likely we will go along with what they think, like, or ask of us.

Persistence – Sometimes persuasion is in the form of persistence by continuing to ask for what they want, or talking fast and including a lot of information (this can sometimes feel like "word salad" when the person includes a lot of words jumbled together, that don't always go together coherently).

"*Correlation does not necessarily imply Causation*" – That is a fancy way of saying that just because two things happen together, does not mean that one caused the other. Sometimes a person who is trying to persuade others will deliberately confuse correlation and causation. It is often used to generate emotion and convince people to take some form of action, purchase a product, etc. For instance, a commercial that portrays happy people having a good time while they use a certain product, implies that this product creates happiness and fun.

Part 3 – Healing and Recovery

Chapter 9: Self-Care

The first and most important action to take to protect yourself and respond the best way you can when you have been the survivor of a scam or fraud is to take care of yourself.

Please don't underestimate this.

The more you achieve balance among all areas of your life (work/school, social, family, personal, etc.), and care for your personal self along with your family and others that are important to you, the more resilient you will be and the more personal energy and resources you will have.

Self-care looks different for each of us. You are the best judge on what your own self-care could be and what works best. It encompasses many things, including having strong and healthy boundaries.

You might think of self-care activities as being in four general areas:

- Take care of your physical body

- Don't overdo it - know your limits

- Do things you enjoy and that replenish your energy

- Have strong and healthy boundaries

There is more detail below about these areas of self-care.

Take Care of Your Physical Body

The most basic of self-care activities are those that take good care of your physical body.

- Eat in a healthy way that fits you the best. Learn about nutrition, eat balanced meals, pay attention to how certain foods affect you, and have fun with new recipes.

- Develop an activity plan that fits your lifestyle, age, and capabilities. Determine the right amount of activity for you with your doctor.

- Get the right amount of sleep to fit you the best. Sometimes we underestimate the importance of getting enough sleep to be able to function at our best. This helps you both physically and mentally.

Don't Overdo It - Know Your Limits

It is also important to know when you are overextending yourself and life is out of balance.

- Take things slowly when you can

- Tackle difficulties one at a time

- Plan and organize your days to avoid getting overwhelmed

- Every day, take time to do something you enjoy even if it is only for a few minutes

Do Things You Enjoy and That Replenish Your Energy

The list of self-care activities below is a long one, and that is on purpose. Not all of these will appeal to you. A variety of activities are included so that hopefully at least a few of them will appeal to most people, and some of these ideas can spark other activity ideas that may work for you.

- Practice deep breathing - in through your nose and out through your mouth

- Draw, paint, or another creative activity you enjoy

- Call a friend or family member who supports you

- Plant a flower, do some gardening

- Listen to music

- Write in a journal

- Take a walk

- Ride a bike

- Read a good book

- Do something nice for someone else

- Watch a funny or inspirational movie

- Explore the Internet (YouTube, Facebook, Instagram) for funny, inspirational, or interesting videos

- Laugh! Humor is an excellent coping skill

- Play with a pet

- Go to church, or engage in a spiritual activity

- Listen to a guided imagery recording, or create your own

- Write a list of qualities you like about yourself

- Dance to your favorite music

- Do yoga

- Sit in the sun and close your eyes

- Cut pictures out of magazines and make a collage or a vision board

- Read the comics

- Put on your favorite good smelling lotion

- Do a puzzle

- Put an inspirational quote up on your bathroom mirror

- Draw with sidewalk chalk

- Slowly eat one piece of your favorite candy or treat

- Play a musical instrument

- Draw random designs and color them in

- Start a blog

- Organize one part of your house - a room, a closet, a drawer…

- Do a different kind of workout you've been wanting to try

- Write a thank you card to someone you've been meaning to thank for something important

- Play a computer or video game

- Meditate

- Pray

- Read an inspirational book

- Do one thing towards a personal goal you have

- Have you been dreaming about doing something that is meaningful to you, is on your bucket list, or is in line with your purpose? Do just one thing related to that.

- Take some time to be alone, or just do NOTHING

- Join a Meetup group or other organization that is aligned with one of your interests

- Do a grounding exercise such as 5-4-3-2-1: What are five things you see? What are four things you hear? What are three things you feel? (tactile such as warm/cold, a breeze, the chair you are sitting in, etc.) What are two things you smell? And if it applies, what is something you taste? Depending on the circumstances, you can change what senses go with which number.

- Do a mindfulness exercise

- Download a relaxation app on your smart phone and do one of the activities

- Consider activities that could help you get rid of some anger such as an anger room (smashing plates or other objects) or a boxing class

- Participate in local government or other organizations to support change that stops scammers (Think *Mothers Against Drunk Drivers* which began out of the pain of a group of mothers who had lost children to drunk drivers)

A few additional ideas about self-care:

- If you can, it may help to dedicate a place in your home to quiet, relaxing, self-care activities. If you have a space dedicated to this, it may be that when you enter this space you automatically begin to relax and feel better.

- When you are with friends or family, only attune with people you want to attune with (the "feel good" people) and do this mindfully. When we attune with someone, and you might think of it as feeling very connected with someone, humans tend to mirror each other. Body movements happen at the same time, such as leaning towards each other, or holding your body in a similar position. Observe how much you mirror the other person or how much they mirror you. This feels even better when you notice it!

- Resilience - All of these activities build your resilience and your energy reserves. This allows you to bring your best self to dealing with someone toxic in your life.

Boundaries

Boundaries are not always the first thing that people think of when they think of self-care. I tend to think of this as one of the most important aspects of self-care, however. Boundaries are your way of letting others know what is and is not all right with you. Let's think about boundaries in three general areas:

- Physical boundaries

- Relational/social boundaries (how you are treated by others)

- Energetic boundaries (your time, the energy you put into something)

In the context of healing when you have been scammed, it may be even more important than usual for you to think about what your own boundaries need to be. You may need to have stronger than usual boundaries after being hurt by this scam for some amount of time, and that is all right. *Trusted people in your life will understand this and will not try to get you to change your boundaries, they will support them.*

Most scams are all about breaking down relational/social boundaries and getting you to do something you wouldn't typically do. To some extent, energetic boundaries are broken as well; pushing for more energy and time from you will make it more likely that you change your relational/social boundaries and associated behavior.

If you feel like working on your own boundaries would be helpful, there are many resources in the form of books, articles and websites.

Chapter 10: Protecting Yourself in the Future

Feeling that you can protect yourself in the future will be an important aspect of your own healing. This will bring a feeling of empowerment and begin to reduce the self-doubt you have experienced.

Educate Yourself

This book may be a good start to educate yourself on different forms of scams, however, its purpose is to help you with the effects this crime has had on you personally and not to educate. For instance, Appendix A provides a very high-level list of types of scam and fraud for easy reference only.

An excellent Internet resource on types of scams is available from Les Henderson at the website https://www.crimes-of-persuasion.com, or his book of the same title, *Crimes of Persuasion: Schemes, Scams, Frauds*[8].

It is important to stay current on this topic. You can expect scammers to keep on changing the things they do to attempt to steal from people.

Practice Recognizing Forms of Manipulation, Psychological Biases, Cognitive Distortions, and Persuasion Techniques

After reviewing these tactics in this book, you might consider some practice at recognizing them. I think this may be taken as an odd recommendation. I'm writing this from the idea that there is a lot in our world that we can't control, and we can reduce anxiety and the effects of traumas such as this one when we "take care of" the things we can control. Practicing, or paying attention to these techniques, is something you can control.

I don't mean any kind of formal sit-down to study and practice, by the way. The idea is to have it in the back of your mind to pay attention to the techniques used when you realize a person is trying to persuade another to do something; this may be something you observe on television or in a movie, or when you are listening to a salesperson.

The more easily you can name a form of manipulation, a bias, or a cognitive distortion, the more easily you can resist allowing it to influence you. You increase your ability to choose how to respond to others the more you know about how these are used in persuasion.

Report the Crime

If you have been reluctant to report a scam or fraud to the appropriate authorities, you are not alone. It has been difficult to report statistics on scams and fraud that are perpetrated on individuals, and to conduct research as well, because of the understandable embarrassment and shame that individuals often feel afterwards.

If you are (or possibly are) willing to report the crime against you, however, the result could be a sense of feeling more empowered, even when you feel certain that the person won't be caught. Also, this is another form of action that you have complete control over whether it happens or not.

Responding When You Think it is Another Scam

Unfortunately, scammers share information about survivors so if you have been scammed once, there is a strong possibility that scammers will attempt again. Thinking about how you will respond if you suspect another scam is also something within your control.

The following ideas are presented for you to consider, and to think about what fits your situation and your personality best. While not listed, a very easy, go-to response is to hang up on a caller you suspect is a scammer or deleting an email that is suspicious.

If the scam you are a survivor of was a romance scam, the following ideas could be particularly useful. Because that type of scam is relatively personal compared to others, you may still be working through feelings you have for the (fictitious) person, which can make it more difficult to say no.

It may be easier for you to "follow a script" rather than respond spontaneously. After reviewing these ideas below, creating a phrase or two to use when you feel pressured may help you feel more confident.

Say "Stop" - Seems obvious, right? It is included here because this may be something you resort to if other responses fail to change the situation, or that you say in combination with one of the other approaches. For some of us, however, this is a difficult thing to do. For instance, if you are a woman and were raised to be a "good girl" and "be nice," standing up for yourself or advocating for yourself goes against that. If you want to try this anyway, practicing with a trusted and supportive person can help.

"Broken Record" – This is another response that you may eventually resort to when others fail. It is when you repeat the same exact phrase each time you respond to someone, such as when maintaining a boundary. After responding, if the person keeps pushing to have the conversation now, you can simply repeat a phrase such as, "I won't do that," to each of their attempts to get you to agree.

Wait/Buy Time - It is all right to say, "I'll think about it and let you know." Sometimes, particularly if you are feeling some pressure to say yes, waiting before you commit helps you to more thoroughly think about the impact of saying yes to a request, and it gives you time to discuss it with a trusted person.

"Call Out" or "Name" Manipulative Behavior - You may choose to respond to someone by naming what you are feeling at the moment and naming the behavior that is happening between the two of you. Some possible statements may be:

"You say this isn't a scam, but I don't believe you."

"It seems like my feelings are being minimized right now."

"I feel like you are trying to rush me, so that I don't have time to think about whether this is okay or not."

Grey Rock/Don't Respond – Choosing this response means that you basically DON'T respond emotionally. You pretend to be a "grey rock" – boring, not changing, no emotion. A rock doesn't get upset and it doesn't jump up and fix things when there is a problem.

This is another response or approach that you may have to resort to, it would be after other attempts fail.

Occasionally, someone will tell me that this response feels weak. If you have ever tried it, however, you probably found that it actually takes a tremendous amount of strength, patience, and perseverance. With some people and some situations, there is nothing you can do or say to make it better, and if being a 'grey rock 'helps you cope in that moment, and could potentially reduce how much a situation escalates, it is a great response.

No Explanation Needed – The idea of not having to explain or excuse why you want or need to act in a certain way is an important one. It is also another mental exercise you do to prepare when you expect a problem to come up, and also as an ongoing reminder to keep yourself in an empowered state.

There are many times when you offer an explanation for the way you feel. With trusted people in your life, this is a part of connecting, understanding, and knowing each other. However, when I have emphasized that you don't need to explain yourself, it is for the times when there is a sense of needing to justify why you feel the way you do.

This need could be coming from something about you that drives you to want to explain yourself; and it could also be from another person who demands an explanation for the purpose of trying to convince you to do something else. It may even be an implication that your feelings must measure up in some way to be valid enough to warrant needing a certain action. And there is a sense of the other person feeling they have a right to approve or disapprove of your need. This simply isn't true; instead, it is an effort to manipulate you and get you to change what you are doing.

Disengage - If a conversation becomes contentious or even more pressured, disengaging is withdrawing and refusing to engage in a power struggle. You might calmly state that you are not willing to argue, discuss who is right or wrong, or another statement that fits the situation.

Other words and actions may essentially express the same thing. The "broken record" or "grey rock" responses are both ways to disengage from a difficult or contentious situation.

When you refuse to argue, hopefully, then there is no reason for the other person to continue arguing. These statements also do not indicate that you agree, or that you are going to change your perspective.

Holding Energetic Boundaries

Holding energetic boundaries could be seen as a specific part of managing relational/social boundaries; I talk about it separately because in dealing with difficult people such as scammers, it is useful to know how this type of boundary can be broken and used to take advantage of you.

This is about choosing and controlling how much energy or time you put into thoughts, emotions, people, and situations; and as mentioned in the chapter about self-care, breaching your energy boundaries relentlessly can wear you down and cause you to allow your relational/social boundaries to change.

It can sometimes seem impossible to withhold your personal energy when you want to or need to. This may be particularly true for you if you identify yourself in any of these ways:

- An empath, or very empathic

- A highly sensitive person

- A people pleaser

- A helping professional

It becomes even more difficult to hold your energy separate from another person when you are in a relationship with someone who is manipulative. A manipulative person can draw energy from you in various ways.

This phrase is an important one in thinking about holding energetic boundaries:

"Manage your emotional uptake from another person."

I want to focus on how you do that. Use the ideas listed in the upcoming sections to help you find strategies that work for you to manage your own energetic boundaries.

Self-Talk

These self-talk ideas are centered on the way you think about yourself, the world and others. They are mental exercises. The emotions we feel are a result of the way we think and also a result of beliefs that we hold.

By challenging beliefs you hold and looking for alternate ways of thinking about something, you are likely to change the emotions you have about yourself, a person, or a situation. You also are better equipped to manage emotions that may arise.

These ideas are also focused on encouraging you to achieve a detached and peaceful mental state when you are in a difficult situation. This allows you some emotional distance from the manipulative efforts of someone toxic.

Some of these are statements and some are ideas. Any one of them may help you get into a mental state that allows you to participate in a conversation or situation, but not take on as much pain, or have your energy drained, as much as you have in the past.

Ideally, you keep practicing the things out of this list that work well for you, and eventually you will have a great deal of conscious control over how much of your emotional energy you allow to be depleted.

- Care, but do not carry.

- Observe, but do not absorb.

- Don't let another person's emotions merge with yours.

- Ask yourself, "Do I want to allow this into my life, or don't I?"

- "Serve from the saucer" or "give from the overflow." The idea is that if you give from what you hold in your cup, it is diminishing what you need for yourself. However, if you give from what overflows from your cup (into the saucer), you are giving out of the abundance you possess, and it doesn't harm you to give it.

- Sarah Knight's book, *The Life-Changing Magic of Not Giving a F*ck*[9] is a good resource to help you decide what is worth giving your energy to, and what isn't.

- Don't take things personally. Although a manipulative person will often try to get you to feel as if a statement or action on their part is personal towards you, if you can avoid taking it on in that way, it will help. In *The Four Agreements*[10], not taking things personally is one of the four agreements that Don Miguel Ruiz writes about. The core idea is that what any other person says or does is not about you - it is about them. It is based on their experience of the world, and their perspective. They may say something about you and direct it towards you and it is still about that other person.

- Ask yourself, "What else might be true?" This question lets you begin to see other possible explanations and can decrease or change your own emotional response. You may be like me, and you tend to develop a story about what is happening in a situation. The story might be based on past experiences of yours that are completely unrelated to the situation, or beliefs you hold.

- Accept that some people will not respect your boundaries, no matter what you do. This is a difficult state to get to at times, especially when you don't have any positive options if the person doesn't respect your boundaries.

If a concept or phrase from this section appeals to you, making it a mantra may be helpful. For instance, three phrases that are often helpful are: "It is what it is," "It won't feel like this forever," and "It isn't my job to fix this." When a phrase is meaningful and easy to remember, using it as a mantra can be a calming and hopeful way of coping in a difficult moment.

Imagery

There are several possible ways of using imagery to both hold on to your own emotional energy, as well as block another person's emotional energy from getting to you. Although these are imaginary, many people find these helpful. Remember, you can always adjust or combine these ideas to fit you and what is meaningful to you.

- Bubble - Imagine a bubble all around you. You can imagine this in whatever form is most meaningful to you. For instance, the bubble could be invisible, or you might imagine it to be shimmering, such as how Glenda the Good Witch of the North appears and leaves in the movie, *The Wizard of Oz*[11]. Or, the bubble can be multicolored, a certain color, or something else. You are in complete control over what goes in or out of the bubble. When I use this, I imagine other people's emotions, words, or energy bouncing off the bubble and that those things can't get to me unless I let them in.

- Shield - You could also imagine a shield between you and the other person, for instance, the shield of a Viking shield-maiden. The same idea applies, nothing gets through the shield unless you decide it can. For me, this image carries a lot of strength, courage, and vitality and those qualities help it work well for me. I mean, shield-maidens were badasses, right?

- Kevlar® - Some people imagine they are wearing a Kevlar® vest to protect themselves from another person's emotions or energy. I feel like this can be very symbolic as well. One of the most important things that Kevlar® protects is your heart, and with boundaries you are often protecting your "heart" as well.

- Teflon® - Imagining that you are covered in Teflon® is another thing that people use to protect themselves. Nothing sticks to Teflon®, right? So another person's words, emotions, and energy bounce or slide right off.

- Another image that is a protective one similar to those above is imagining a "force field" all around you that protects you from others' energy. Again, you have complete control over this field. If you want to allow positive energy to get to you, great.

- Wind - You can imagine that the other person's words, energy, or emotions flow around you like the wind, and they do not stay with you.

- River or Creek - You can imagine that you are standing in a river or creek and any energy from another person that gets absorbed by accident flows out of you, into the water, and is carried away down the stream.

- Observer/Dual Awareness - Sometimes you can detach or withdraw from the emotions or energy coming at you from someone if you go into a dual state of awareness that is one part of you and your mind participating in the conversation, with another part of your mind observing what is happening. In the observing part of your awareness, it often works well if you picture that you are watching yourself and the other person on a movie screen, television screen, or device screen. Sometimes people picture the scene as if they are passing it on a train or in a car. And sometimes people picture it as if they are a fly on a wall.

- Protective Persona or Animal - Is there an animal or persona you connect with that represents the protection you need? For instance, a bear is often perceived as a protective spirit and could be imagined to be protecting you in a difficult moment. Other beings may be used in this way as well, such as a superhero or a fictional character that is meaningful to you. This protective spirit may walk beside you at times, or stand with you. Or you may ask yourself what this persona would do in a situation and let that guide you.

- Container - You may find it useful to imagine a container of some kind such as a box, a chest that has multiple locks on it, a suitcase, or another type of container that is meaningful to you. You can then imagine that either your emotions are "compartmentalized" in this container until later when it is a more productive time to deal with them; or you can imagine that the other person's emotions are held in this container and cannot get to you.

Actions

As mentioned previously, self-care is an important action to take. Self-care builds up your reserves to protect yourself and to respond the best way you can with difficult people.

In addition to taking care of yourself physically and mentally with self-care, consider trying one or more of the following activities to protect your energy and build your resilience:

- Take the time to evaluate whether you lean more towards introversion or extraversion. Look back at how you have felt after social gatherings of different sizes, as well as how you have felt after long periods of being alone. Are you energized and feel ready to take on more if you have had plenty of time alone? Or is it spending time with others that gives you lots of energy? And be careful to consider who you are with - some people are more draining than others. Knowing this about yourself helps you to plan your days, your weeks, and more. If you identify as an introvert, you may need "alone time" every day to help build your energy back up.

- Say no. Review parts of your life and in particular the times when your energy is drained, and look for ways that you can start to say no. Start small, it is easier that way; i.e., start with things that aren't as important to others that may be disappointed.

- Consider areas where you could accept help from others, or even ask for help. For many of us, it is just as difficult to say no to some things as it is to accept help for some things. We all need help once in a while, though. Start small with this one as well. It might be as small as letting another one of the parents at your kids' school help you carry all those art supplies out to your car. You don't have to carry them all yourself! Then, work your way up to getting help with things that are more important. It *feels good* to reciprocate in this way with people who help you, and accept help from you as well.

- Choose carefully when you empathize and attune with a person. Attunement is allowing yourself to match the emotional state of another person. This ability is an important part of how we connect with another person; however, sometimes you do not want to do this, such as when a person is extremely angry or excessively critical. An exercise that may work to help you gain control over how much empathy you feel (when you don't want to) is to practice increasing feelings of empathy and then bringing them back down. Do this several times, and then practice decreasing feelings of empathy and see if you can feel a difference.

- Journal. Although journaling is also self-care and is one path towards healing that will be discussed more in Chapter 11, it can also help you plan and strategize alternative ways to respond.

- Notice the activities that help you feel more resilient and things that replenish your energy and build you up. Self-awareness is a tremendous strength. You will also notice the activities that do the opposite of course. As you notice more and more, you will begin to structure your daily routines and how you spend your time in general, to take better care of yourself.

- Rehearse what you might say in a situation where you expect someone to drain your energy, or push your boundaries. Sometimes, stepping through a moment you anticipate can help you dispel the emotion associated with it. It can be useful to see the situation similar to a chess game, where you must think several moves ahead, and anticipate what the other person will do. (Chess is more predictable than people are though!) When you expect it, the impact is less, and you are better prepared to respond in a healthier way than you might have otherwise.

- Name what is happening. If you find yourself in a situation that is draining your energy, if you can "name it" and describe what is happening that will often allow you to "shut off" the energy it is taking from you. For instance, noticing a salesperson at the door leaves most of us with a feeling of dread and annoyance, anticipating what may happen (will the person be pushy?). Name what you notice, mentally decide to shut off the energy you might have put into that situation, and you'll use up less of your energy overall.

- Build your self-worth. Your self-worth and sense of your own value can be damaged by being scammed, being manipulated, and it can be affected by trauma as well. Explore ways to build your self-worth to strengthen your sense of self, your resilience, and your ability to respond to difficult situations with an empowered state of being.

- Build your self-control. Take care to examine ways that you may be sabotaging yourself. When you have been scammed, it can be very easy to turn to less healthy and even destructive habits that undermine your ability to cope. If your go-to coping skills include binge-watching Netflix until late at night and interrupting healthy sleep patterns, or using substances or food to soothe yourself, consider taking action to change those habits.

Chapter 11: Healing

Being the survivor of a scam of any kind often leaves a person with the effects of trauma. You may not have thought of this as trauma before now and if that fits your experience, healing is possible.

Seeing it as trauma does not make you weak. Actually, the opposite is true; it can help you in the healing process to see it this way and that leads to strength and resilience. When a person tries to push this idea away, though, and internally says, "It wasn't that bad" or "I shouldn't be having this much trouble getting past it," it can delay the healing process.

This chapter is full of ideas about healing. You probably won't need to work on or incorporate all of these. Honor your own unique healing process and choose what feels important to you. Over time, you may feel that one or another of these is what you need to work on. This can change over time.

You will also find that at least some of these overlap a bit or you can use them together. For instance, "Challenge Unhelpful Beliefs" is an idea that can be used along with many of the other healing ideas and activities listed here.

It seems important that this chapter contains all of the suggested healing activities for you, so you may notice that some of the ideas listed here were mentioned previously in this book.

I've separated these ideas into three broad categories: Change in Thought/Emotion Skills; Concepts to Explore; and Actions.

Change in Thought/Emotion Skills

Self-Awareness - This is a skill that you can improve. It is also a skill that is absolutely essential to personal growth. Most likely, you are already very self-aware. However, if you want to improve this skill, mindfulness or meditation are likely to help.

Telling Your Story – We all have a "story" we tell about our life, our self, and it incorporates many beliefs about people and the world we live in. And this changes over time. The story you are telling yourself now about what has happened to you is going to be different at some point. The phrase that is commonly used to describe this in current times is "change the narrative." I love this phrase. It is empowering.

The changes happen out of maturity, out of learning, or possibly out of gaining new information. Journaling can help you tell this story, and at the same time just noticing how you are telling the story to yourself is important, and gives you an opportunity to mindfully change how you are telling it.

For instance, if you keep saying to yourself how stupid you are for being fooled by this person, perhaps this is an area where you begin to change the narrative.

Allow Yourself to Grieve – This was covered in some detail in a previous chapter. It is worth noting again that giving yourself permission to grieve is important. Sometimes it is helpful to make a list of the things you are grieving. Insights may come from this process that help, such as additional things you are grieving that you weren't aware of before.

Particularly when the scam was a romance scam, it is all right to honor the positive memories you carry related to this, too. One aspect of the grieving process is to integrate all parts of what has happened into our personal narrative.

Allow Yourself to Feel and Express Anger - Being the survivor of a scam is likely to have left you feeling angry. You probably have plenty of things you are angry with the other person for, as well as possibly being angry with yourself (for "putting up with it" or staying so long). Just like with grief above, giving yourself permission or freedom to feel anger is important, too. With anger, however, it can have a lot of power over you when it isn't expressed in some way. Expressing it in a healthy way and allowing it to exist takes away some of that power, and allows the anger to begin to dissipate.

Words may be enough for you to express your anger in a healthy way, such as talking about it with a supportive person in your life, or journaling about it. Some people need a physical outlet, too. You might need to go somewhere alone and scream or cry, you might punch a pillow, or you might (safely!) need to destroy something.

Self-Worth – When you've been the survivor of a scam, your self-worth takes a big hit. Start being boldly realistic about your strengths and values. Yes, you aren't perfect, and the more realistic you are about who you are and how you are, the more you will appreciate the gifts you bring to people in your life and the world.

Something you might find helpful in working on this is to take the 240 question VIA (Values in Action) Survey of Character Strengths[12] questionnaire you can find at this website: https://www.authentichappiness.sas.upenn.edu. Create a login and then look under "Questionnaires" to find it. Once you answer the questions, the results are 24 character strengths in the order of importance for you. I've found that when people do this, they gain a new appreciation for what is important to them and why.

Trust Your Gut – This is another thing that takes a hit when you've been scammed. You stop trusting your gut (trusting your intuition or insight). It takes some time to start trusting yourself again in this regard. Practice. Try. You can gain your confidence back.

Guilt or Shame Versus Self-Acceptance – You may be feeling the burden of shame or guilt. You may beat yourself up about how you handled the entire situation with the scammer, or only a part of it, or that you keep acting in a way that doesn't fit with how you see yourself. If you can become aware of when shame or guilt is overtaking you, and challenge the beliefs associated with it, you can increase self-acceptance.

Each time you notice when shame or guilt is coming up and challenge it, you become more authentic and true to yourself.

Forgiving Yourself – You know how people tend to say that the hardest person to forgive is yourself? "They" seem to be correct! Many people struggle the hardest to forgive themselves. This is another area to challenge beliefs. Do you even need to forgive yourself? Were you doing your best? Stepping back and looking at the situation or regrets you have in a boldly realistic way can help you challenge the beliefs that are keeping you from forgiving yourself.

Forgive Others - It may also be difficult to forgive the person or the people who scammed you. It may take a lot of time.

You also don't *have to* forgive that person; this is your choice. It is very much a cliché that forgiveness is for the person who does the forgiving. And yet, it is also very true. This thought always reminds me of a Lily Tomlin quote: "Forgiveness means giving up all hope for a better past." The process of forgiving allows you to let go of what has happened, and what you cannot change.

Keep in mind that forgiving definitely does not mean that you are excusing what happened, or letting that person off the hook.

Forgiving is supposed to mean that you let go of the need to hold on to the anger and other toxic emotions associated with what happened.

Challenge Unhelpful Beliefs – Each of us hold an immeasurable number of beliefs. In general, those beliefs are about our self, others, and the world. Some are conscious, and some are subconscious beliefs. These beliefs begin forming very early in life as a result of our observations, what other people say, and what we experience both in the world and with other people.

In challenging unhelpful beliefs, one part of the work is discovering what subconscious beliefs you may hold. A lot of the time, we aren't aware of the belief or that it is having such a big influence. Once you are aware of a belief, you then have the ability to challenge it.

An example of a subconscious belief might be a child that has spent most of their time up to a certain point with parents and other caregivers who treat the child with love and care. Up to that time, the child believes that people are safe and give you love. At some point soon after a child begins to interact with others outside of this small number of people, this changes. The child will eventually encounter someone who is harsh, hurtful, or mean towards the child. The child has to adjust their belief - now they believe that not all people are loving or caring, some are mean or hurtful.

A belief about how others behave will evolve as a person matures, depending on the experiences and observations of that person.

One belief that is important when you have been scammed is that before the scam, you may not have ever questioned your level of intelligence, but now you are questioning it after this has happened. Hopefully this book has given you information that helps you challenge the unhelpful thoughts that have begun to come up for you.

Pay attention to the specific thoughts that come up in your mind. The questions below will hopefully help you decide what is a more realistic perspective about yourself, the world, or other people. Not every question will apply, but as you identify beliefs to challenge, consider one or more of the questions below:

How do I know this is true?

What is the evidence for and against this being true?

Is thinking this way a habit, or is it fact?

Am I including all of the important information related to this?

Could I be thinking in an "all-or-nothing" way?

Am I taking this to an extreme or exaggerating?

Am I focused on just one aspect of this?

How dependable is the source of this information?

Could I be confusing "possible" with "likely"?

Am I basing my conclusion on feelings or facts?

Am I too focused on unrelated parts?

Have I jumped to a conclusion without having all the information I need?

Am I assuming or "mind reading" about what others think, or why they have done something?

It may also be helpful to think about:

How much do I believe this? (possibly on a scale from 0-100%)

What else could be true?

For a belief to form or to change, a person must see evidence, such as through observation and experience. Sometimes that evidence is another person who is an example or role model. And, sometimes that evidence is something you imagine is possible. Look for these things as well when you are trying to change a belief that is holding you back.

Allow Yourself Some Mistakes - You aren't going to change your thinking patterns and feel better right away. This is hard work. Being patient with yourself and knowing that you will need to practice these skills will help you. You may replay situations in your mind, and identify multiple things you should have said or done differently. In the beginning this will be true, but each time you backtrack and replay a situation, and identify where you could have done something differently, you are setting yourself up to behave and think differently in the future.

Identify Cognitive Distortions – When we looked at cognitive distortions previously in this book, the focus was on how those are used to deceive a person in a scam. By bringing it up here, I am asking you to consider how cognitive distortions may be holding you back in your healing process, and to become aware of them and change those thoughts and beliefs.

For instance, "all-or-nothing" thinking is an example of a cognitive distortion. After the scam, your thoughts about how you must be stupid are an example of all-or-nothing thinking. The statement is about your entire self and this can't be true. Find a more accurate statement, and each time you notice this thought coming up for you, replace it with the new thought that is more accurate.

Identify Psychological Biases – As with cognitive distortions, when this was discussed previously, the focus was on how these patterns of thinking could have been used to deceive you. Now, we want to look at how these patterns could be holding you back in your healing efforts and once you are aware of them, change the thoughts and beliefs.

Spirituality - For many people, their faith in something larger than themselves or this moment is healing. Using this strength within yourself in a way that is meaningful to you can help you in your healing process. For instance, if you are Christian, using a

Bible concordance to search for words important in your healing may be a helpful exercise.

Change Your Internal Voice - Many of us can identify an internal voice, and much too often it is a harsh or critical voice. Sometimes, a person can identify another specific person that is speaking in that voice in your head. If this voice is critical or harsh, as you become aware of each time it comes up in your thoughts, imagine that voice *is* different and *is saying* something different.

For instance, a friend of mine sometimes hears her mother's criticism in her head. That voice might say, "You are way too sensitive, you always overreact." She changes the voice to Mr. Rogers and imagines what he would say instead, such as, "It is perfectly okay to let someone know when they have hurt your feelings."

Let this new voice be one that is empowering and kind.

"Contain" It – Use your imagination to create a container in your mind (a plain or decorative box, a cave, a deep hole in the ground, a cabinet or freezer, etc.). When particular thoughts or emotions are bothering you or interrupting your sleep, put the thoughts or emotions in your container and close it up tight. Imagining that these troubling thoughts or emotions are contained can give you some relief from them, even if it is only temporary. And at times, once you essentially give your mind permission to stop working on whatever this is, a solution may present itself.

Concepts to Explore

Fear-Based Versus Love-Based – This is a concept about how you approach things or how you see things – situations, people, even yourself. When you act or decide out of fear, such as not getting back on social media out of fear over what stranger may contact you, you also miss out on connecting with family and friends.

If this is going on for you, reflecting on whether you are making choices and acting out of fear may help you create a change, and lead to acting out of love and feeling more at peace.

Face Your Tendency to Control Others – A defense mechanism that people can develop after a trauma is becoming controlling to some degree. You try to control your environment and others around you to be able to have SOME amount of control over negative things in your life. A person might become hyper-vigilant (excessively watchful about things going on around them), and this can become controlling as you try to anticipate problems and avoid them.

Over time, this can become a habit or tendency in many forms and with many people in your life. When you really think about it, it also doesn't work, does it? Look for ways you may have incorporated this defense mechanism, and look for alternatives that are healthier for you and for others you care about in your life.

Know Your Triggers – "Triggers" are things that tend to upset you, or things that lead to a negative emotional response. And for many people, this will mean things that are associated with the scam in any way are painful.

Knowing your triggers allows you to both heal from the pain and/or trauma of your experiences, and compensate for what feels like an automatic response. For example, if you experience dread and anxiety each time you receive an email from your bank, this is a trigger. It is associated with the money you have lost. Notice it, and mindfully examine it. Doing this allows you to accept that it is a trigger for you and you can then change the outcome. For a while, to give yourself time to work on it, you might turn off email notifications from your bank. The anxiety can diminish, and after some amount of time you can turn the notifications back on, and it won't be a problem.

Triggers are causing a traumatic response. Triggers can sometimes cause an "amygdala hijack" which is essentially when your amygdala takes over brain functioning and takes you into a fight, flight, or freeze response. If this is happening to you, please know that over time it is possible to get control over this. It is normal for this to happen when real danger is present, but in some circumstances the response gets activated when a person is reminded of a trauma (or a time when that person felt in danger). Working with a therapist can speed up the healing process.

Imposter Syndrome – This term is usually used in the context of work performance, but it is similar to when people express fear and self-doubt about being able to function in the world after being scammed.

We all tend to show our best to the world and not talk as much about the challenges and problems, or even secrets, going on in our lives. And this is easy to forget.

It isn't helpful to compare other people's outsides with your insides. Remember that we all have struggles and many other people have been scammed too, possibly even people that you know. Yes, this scam has caused you a lot of pain and you have probably made some mistakes along the way, but that doesn't mean you aren't capable of being a healthy person in your life from here on out.

Keep Striving for Personal Growth – This is very broad, isn't it?? However, it is likely that whatever form of personal growth is going on for you, if you do see yourself as *growing*, self-acceptance and self-worth tend to improve.

Identity Change – How has your identity changed? There are multiple ways to ask this question: how has your identity changed as a result of having had this experience? What are new ways you would describe your identity now after having been through what you've experienced?

The reality is that you are different now. How are you different? You might feel you are more resilient now. You also might feel like you will always have a harder time trusting another person.

Strive to keep a realistic, and also compassionate, view of yourself. Remember your strengths, too. A scam is hard and it is damaging. Give yourself some grace.

Understanding Healthy Attachment - If you experienced a romance scam, exploring what healthy, secure attachment is like and how healthy relationships develop over time will help in your healing process. As you begin to examine beliefs you had before and how they have changed, or beliefs you have now that are affecting relationships in a negative way, you will likely find that those beliefs have been affecting your ability to connect with others. A great resource on attachment is a book titled, *Attached*[14].

Identify any "Stuck" Points - Each of us is prone to getting stuck, emotionally, when a situation is hurtful. Once you identify a "stuck point," you are likely to find an area of this book that can help you resolve any unhelpful beliefs that are keeping you stuck. You might uncover this by thinking about phrases that repeat in your mind, or when you are telling a trusted person in your life about what is happening. Some possible phrases could be:

"If I could just figure out why I didn't see this was a scam, I would feel better." (There's a false sense of control in this)

"Am I over-reacting?" (If you are uncomfortable, there is a reason, either from a belief within you or because of the nature of the experience)

(in a romance scam) "If I could just have been a better person, maybe he wouldn't have gone through with taking my money."

Revenge - No, I don't believe that getting revenge against someone is a healthy healing exercise! It caught your eye, though, didn't it? It is actually a very human response to want revenge of some kind when you have been hurt. Let's put a positive spin on it. Your best "revenge" is to find healing, and to live your life with peace and well-being. When anger comes up and you have thoughts about wanting revenge, try to shift your focus to this concept. Don Miguel Ruiz's book *The Four Agreements*[10] can help with this. It can also be helpful to direct your energy towards making sure the scammer does face appropriate accountability for their actions. This is not about "sticking it to them," it is about preventing them from hurting others.

Strengths and Weaknesses - It can be useful to list your strengths and weaknesses. Doing this can help to identify areas you want to grow as a person, whether that is working on changing a weakness or improving on your strengths. Since it is always easier to identify negatives, you might make a list of your qualities that you consider weaknesses. Once you have that list, try to see how each of those weaknesses can also be a strength or is sometimes a strength.

Creating a list in this way often allows a person to see their qualities more realistically, and then to leverage those strengths in future situations.

Pay It Forward - Paying it forward means that you take what you have experienced and learned, or what you "have," and you give it to another person. You may choose to get involved with an organization that supports people who have survived a scam, or to educate people in some way on how to avoid or spot a scam.

Give Yourself Some Grace - This is a phrase that I use often in my professional work. Far too many people are very hard on themselves, and agonize over mistakes and regrets. For instance, you are allowed to give yourself credit for what you have achieved so far in your healing journey. It is all right to want to get your needs met.

However you achieve it, please find ways to be kind to yourself and give yourself some grace.

You Are A Survivor - I am including this statement with the purpose of encouraging you to cultivate empowerment, avoid feeling like a victim, find your voice, and find new ways to get your needs met in relationships.

You have probably had to adapt to difficult situations very quickly, and learn new methods of coping over time. These qualities mean you have resilience.

Whatever unique form a scam takes, it is very difficult to endure. It has *required* that you be a survivor.

Actions

Self-Care – Although there is an entire chapter on self-care, it is worth mentioning again because it is so important no matter where you are on this journey of healing. Personal growth is hard work and taking care of yourself along the way will make it easier.

Boundaries is one part of self-care.

Taking care of your physical health is another - get the right amount of sleep, nourishment, and movement *for you*.

Activities that are relaxing or somehow beneficial is another part of self-care. For many people, this involves finding things to do that are enjoyable and engaging. Whatever activities you choose, they are all ways to build up your internal emotional and energy resources.

An activity that is not only enjoyable and engaging, but also involves using your senses, can be very grounding and calming when you allow yourself to be fully aware of how it feels. Being by the ocean is a good example; there are strong ocean smells, people often find the vast expanse of the water and beachside to be beautiful, you hear the waves hitting the beach, and you feel the humid air and sand beneath you.

Journaling - This is probably the most common healing activity a counselor suggests, at least in Western cultures. For many people, it is a very effective way to gain personal insight for yourself.

In case journaling hasn't been a helpful activity for you in the past, you might consider trying it a different way. You could try expression via a form of art such as writing song lyrics or poems, it could be talking out loud or even recording yourself talking. The goal is finding a method or medium that works for *you* to gain insight, whatever that may be.

Another idea is to do your journaling in the form of a letter. The letter may be to the person who harmed you, or it could be to your future or past self. Writing a letter to someone is often a very helpful way of processing grief.

You may also find ideas in a book titled, *Journal to the Self: Twenty-Two Paths to Personal Growth*[13] by Kathleen Adams. The author describes twenty-two alternative ways of journaling, for those of us who don't get much out of the stream of consciousness style of journaling that usually comes to mind.

Be With People Who Feel Good – When you start to notice how it feels to spend time with each person in your life, and you stay aware of this through a relationship, I think the potential for connection can be a huge boost in your own healing. Along with that, so can the potential for self-care when you notice that spending time with a particular person drains you more and more as time goes by. Being aware of this and consciously choosing to spend more of your time with people who build you up is great for self-care and healing.

The people that feel good are usually the ones that are most trusted and supportive, too.

Ask For Help – For some people, it is difficult to ask for help. After being scammed, you may be feeling so much shame and embarrassment, you don't want anyone to know, which would also make it difficult to ask for help. However, asking for help is an act of self-care which you need more than ever right now.

Choose a person to ask who is trusted, supportive, and non-judgmental.

If this seems really difficult, start small. Or, consider it practice and keep going until you are good at it. Identify beliefs that may be holding you back, such as, "I don't want to bother _____ with this." In reality, people often feel really good about themselves when they are able to help another person out. Give them the opportunity to feel that way, and ask.

Take Care of Things You Can Control/Let Go of Things You Can't Control - It is common to feel like "everything" is out of your control. It is true that there is a lot out of our control in life, however, when you get in the habit of looking for what you can and can't control, it can do two things:

1) It can give you some level of peace to let go of the things you can't control; you don't have to continue giving as much of your energy to a person or situation by worrying about it, or carrying the general sense of needing to do *something*.

2) It can give you a more constructive way to use your energy, by putting it towards things you can control or do. When you consciously take an action, it is empowering. It gives your energy a direction to go and settles the anxiety over

feeling like you need to do something, because you *are* doing something.

Art and Creativity - Many people find healing in creative activities such as painting, coloring, woodworking, or other tactile art forms. If there is a particular creative activity you enjoy, make time to do that. This is also self-care, but sometimes the meditative quality of some forms of art can help quiet your mind, or bring insights.

For instance, mandalas are often used in art for healing. A mandala is a circular form, often with intricate patterns. You may find that creating a mandala for yourself in a drawing or a painting, or with mosaic tiles for instance is a healing exercise for you. You may want to explore resources to learn about and use mandalas in your own healing journey.

Body-Based Healing – If it appeals to you, you may consider an activity that is body-based, to assist you in your healing process. Some ideas may be engaging in a Restorative Yoga, Yoga Nidra, or other yoga practice; learning a martial art; or making a peaceful walk a part of your routine.

You may also choose to do activities that are simply physically soothing or relaxing on a regular basis.

Letting Go Exercises – There are a few exercises you can do that I refer to as "letting go" exercises. They are physical ways to symbolically relieve yourself of difficult emotions or burdens. In reading this list, you may think of an additional idea that feels good for you, too. With each, the idea is that you create something that has what you want to let go of either in it, on it, as a part of it, etc. And then you destroy that object in some way. Keep safety in mind when you decide how to destroy it!

- Write it out and burn it – journal or write a letter to a person who has harmed you and say ALL of the things you need to say; then burn the pages

- Make an object out of modeling clay or some other creative arts media and then destroy it or burn it

- Smashing plates – get a ceramic dinner plate and a marker, and write all the things you want to let go of on the plate; then find a place to smash the plate into tiny pieces (you might have a "rage room" near you, or you can put the plate into a pillowcase so the pieces are contained and smash it against the ground or use a hammer to destroy it)

- Write the things you want to let go of on a rock (or rocks), and then throw the rock into a body of water, over a cliff, or other symbolic place that is meaningful to you

- Write the things you want to let go of on several rocks, put all the rocks in a backpack; then go for a walk or a hike and really let yourself feel the heaviness and the burden of carrying these around with you; as you progress on your walk or hike, gradually take the rocks out and leave them behind (you can throw them far from the trail, or carefully place them, or whatever is meaningful to you); as you physically lighten the load you are carrying, allow your mind and spirit to also lighten

Join a Group for Support – One very unfortunate thing I have discovered is that there are either no support groups available for people who have been scammed, or there are so few I haven't found one yet. I've been told by a few people that support groups specific to this topic are discouraged, because scammers tend to join them, and attempt to re-victimize people. This is sad, and infuriating.

With this limitation in mind, I included a list of possible alternative support groups to join in Appendix B. Although they aren't on this specific topic, you will still gain emotional support. You may also want to explore other counseling or support group options near you.

Therapy - Working with a trusted therapist can help you take your own personal work beyond what you can do on your own.

Chapter 12: For Family and Friends

For you, a family member or friend of someone who has been the survivor of a scam, I am including this chapter because I know that so many of you will pick up this book to find ways to help the person you care about.

The original article and handout that I wrote long ago, that let me know how much this book was needed, was intended for you as the audience. It was written for a one-hour informational workshop I created for family and friends, because I felt that people who were scammed themselves would not want to attend, out of shame or embarrassment.

Some of the following suggestions could be obvious to you, but are always worth mentioning.

Listen and Empathize Without Judgement

Offering a shoulder to cry on is a no-brainer. But it's important to make your best effort to listen and empathize without judging this person. He is probably already judging himself and beating himself up worse than you ever could, and it is a priceless gift to have someone to talk to who will not judge you for a mistake. People who have been scammed will appreciate someone who listens without judgment while they process what has happened and figure out how to go forward.

Don't Say…

"What were you thinking?"

"How could you be fooled by that?"

"I would never have fallen for that."

"Everybody knows about that scam."

Scammers play on people's emotions, needs, and fears. Sometimes we can be more easily fooled when the scammer presents an easy way to get something we want very badly, or a way to avoid something we are very afraid of. The way our brains tend to work in these situations makes it easier for a scammer to get what they want out of us. Those statements above only bring on even more embarrassment, shame, and self-doubt.

Remind Your Loved One Frequently: "You Are Not Stupid"

Scammers are *extremely good* at what they do. They use tactics based in human psychology and sociology to get people to miss important clues that something is not as it seems. They use the tactics detailed in Part 2 of this book. Scammers often sound very friendly and concerned about the person they are trying to scam.

It is important to encourage the person you care about to look at the situation differently, perhaps more realistically, and determine what made her vulnerable. Which tactics were used? It isn't helpful or accurate to conclude that she "must be so stupid" if she fell for a scam.

Focus on What <u>Can</u> Be Done

It is very common for someone who is in (or has been in) a very difficult situation to think endlessly about all the things they wish they would have done differently. People get emotionally "stuck" in this sometimes, and for many reasons can't get out of this unhelpful thought pattern.

Encourage them to focus their energy on the things they can control, not the things they can't. One thing that tends to help a person get "unstuck" is to take some kind of action to make things better, no matter how small it is. For instance, if the person you care about feels better by:

- Getting educated on scam tactics such as forms of manipulation, psychological biases, and cognitive distortions to prevent being scammed again, or

- Getting involved with an organization that supports people who have been scammed, or

- Reporting the crime

...then encourage them to do it. These are positive actions that help people heal. They are also focused on the future instead of the past, which can help shift a person's attitude to see the situation as a lesson learned and a mistake, instead of feeling like a failure, or stupid, or ruined, which are all common thought patterns after a scam.

Encourage Your Loved One to Forgive Themselves

I think this has been the hardest thing to achieve for clients I have worked with. The person who was scammed may feel like a "complete failure" in life after realizing what has happened. It is easy to lose sight of the fact that although the consequences may be harsh, it is still a mistake and not a statement about the person as a whole. We all make mistakes at times. Encourage self-forgiveness and self-compassion, these can bring healing and peace of mind.

Remember These Factors

- Many people are traumatized when they are scammed. Some situations have a relatively small impact on a person's life, while some people have a harsh or devastating experience. If either you or your loved one consider this experience to have been trauma, please encourage them to find a counselor who is skilled in helping people heal after a traumatic experience.

- In a romance scam, the person is still possibly trying to separate the fictitious person from the perpetrator. This is a difficult process, as it involves grieving for the relationship, what should have been, and the loss of the person they thought they were in a relationship with. Ask your loved one about this. In other words, don't tell them this is happening. When you ask and let them guide you, it is more empowering. Each person will grieve and process situations like this in their own way and in their own time.

- As with grieving and processing what has happened, it will also take time for your loved one to change their view about relationships in the future and trust others again.

- If there was a significant financial impact, the person may also need to revise future plans, their personal will, their lifestyle, and more. Be sensitive to this. Depending on your relationship, this may be something you can or need to help with. There will be grief, processing, and healing from this as well.

Chapter 13: Concluding Thoughts

My hope for you is that you have found something of value in this book to help you heal from what has happened to you. I have witnessed the effects of being scammed many times. While I know that this is possible to overcome, I also know that this takes a tremendous amount of personal strength, perseverance, and care.

Appendix A: Types of Scams

The following information is a relatively simple list of the types of scams. Unfortunately, this list will always be incomplete. New ways of stealing from others are always being thought up by unscrupulous people.

Use this list to seek out resources on the different types of scams, and educate yourself. The websites in Appendix B are resources to research scams and fraud as well.

- Romance and relationship scams

- Employment scams

- Misrepresented as government or authority figure scams (IRS, warrant for your arrest)

- Overpayment scams (targeting anyone selling something or engaging in an exchange of money with someone you don't really know)

- Phishing scams (email or caller appears to be a reputable source but isn't, trying to get personal information for identity theft)

- Investment scams

- Fake products, prizes, sweepstakes, refunds

- Advance fee scams

- Fake computer problems/ransomware

Appendix B: Resources

Support Groups:

Since there are so few support groups specifically for people who have been scammed, when you look for counseling or support groups in your area, also consider those that are focused on trauma or crime victims.

You may also find groups on Facebook or online forums. Please be cautious, scammers may attempt to join these groups and re-victimize people.

You may also be able to find groups or additional support (that isn't made public) when contacting a fraud assistance organization or law enforcement.

You can search the following sites for groups located near you:

- Mental Health America's Support Groups page: https://www.mhanational.org/find-support-groups

- National Alliance on Mental Illness Support Groups page: https://www.nami.org/Support-Education/Support-Groups

- Some therapist directories include group information or the ability to search for a counseling or support group

- A United Kingdom resource for mental health support when you have been the victim of a crime is Victim Support: https://www.victimsupport.org.uk

Law Enforcement/Crime Victim Support:

It may be difficult to figure out where to report the crime against you, or how. The following government or law enforcement sites can help you determine what would be best for you:

United States Federal Trade Commission (FTC): https://www.usa.gov/stop-scams-frauds

United States Federal Bureau of Investigation (FBI): https://www.fbi.gov/scams-and-safety

International Consumer Protection group econsumer.gov that allows you to report international scams: https://www.econsumer.gov/

In the United Kingdom, Action Fraud takes reports of cybercrimes: https://www.actionfraud.police.uk

In addition, it may be best to also report to your local law enforcement organization. An officer or advocate will often be willing to help you determine if this is appropriate or not. Even if the crime is not reported to your local law enforcement, you can ask about resources in your community for victims of a crime.

If a scammer has misrepresented themselves as a member of an organization such as a government agency, business, etc., please also report the incident to that organization; also do this if you receive an email, telephone call, or text from an organization and you do not respond (i.e., a scam didn't actually happen).

Books/Websites:

Crimes of Persuasion website – An extensive resource on types of scams/fraud, victim resources, and more; website owner is Les Henderson who is the author of a book with the same title, *Crimes of Persuasion: Schemes, Scams, Frauds: How con artists will steal your savings and inheritance through telemarketing fraud, investment schemes, and consumer scams*: https://www.crimes-of-persuasion.com/

Multiple articles, ways to find community resources, and more resources for fraud victims: http://www.fraudaid.com

American Association of Retired Persons (AARP) Fraud Watch Network: Articles and other resources to educate yourself, learn how to report, sign up for free alerts, and more resources: https://www.aarp.org/money/scams-fraud/

References

1. Whitty, M. (2013). The scammers persuasive techniques model: Development of a stage model to explain the online dating romance scam. *The British Journal of Criminology, 53(4),* 665-684.

2. Van D. J., Reisch, W., Balderston, J. L., Cukor, G., Hornblow, A., Boyer, C., Bergman, I., ... Warner Home Video (Firm). (2004). *Gaslight.* Burbank, Calif: Warner Home Video.

3. Wilson, Cathy. *Boundaries of steel: A workbook for managing and recovering from toxic relationships.* (2020). Littleton, CO. LifePaths, PLLC.

4. Freyd, J.J. (1997). Violations of power, adaptive blindness, and betrayal trauma theory. *Feminism & Psychology, 7,* 22-32.

5. Henderson, Les. *Crimes of Persuasion: Schemes, Scams, Frauds: How con artists will steal your savings and*

inheritance through telemarketing fraud, investment schemes, and consumer scams. (2003). Azilda, Ontario, Canada: Coyote Ridge Publishing.

6. Knight, Sarah. *The life-changing magic of not giving a f*ck: How to stop spending time you don't have with people you don't like doing things you don't want to do.* (2015). New York, NY: Little, Brown and Company.

7. Ruiz, Don Miguel. *The four agreements: A practical guide to personal freedom (A Toltec wisdom book).* (2018). San Rafael, CA. Amber-Allen Publishing.

8. Baum, L. F. (1939). The wizard of Oz. Hollywood, Calif.: Metro Goldwyn Mayer.

9. Seligman, M. E. P., Ph.D. and Peterson, Christopher. (2005). VIA (Values in Action) Survey of Character Strengths. Retrieved from https://www.authentichappiness.sas.upenn.edu.

10. Adams, Kathleen. *Journal to the self: Twenty-two paths to personal growth.* (1990). New York, NY. Warner Books Inc.

11. Levine, Amir and Heller, Rachel S, F. *Attached: The new science of adult attachment and how it can help you find—and keep—love.* (2011). New York, NY. Penguin Random House LLC.

About Cathy Wilson

Cathy Wilson, LPC, ACS, is the Director of LifePaths Counseling Center, a group of counselors in Littleton, Colorado. She received her degree in Community Counseling from Regis University in Denver, and has been providing counseling services for more than ten years. Cathy is an active member of several mental health communities such as local consultation groups and the American Counseling Association; and she is also an Approved Clinical Supervisor.

In 2018, she began conducting workshops on creating a professional will for mental health practitioners, and soon after this, wrote her first book titled *One Last Act* to help colleagues complete this important task. She wrote her second book, *Boundaries of Steel*, after creating and facilitating groups with the same name, to help people manage and recover from toxic relationships. *The Emotional Impact of Being Scammed and How to Recover* is her third book.

You can find more information about her and about LifePaths at https://www.lifepathscounseling.com.

Made in the USA
Columbia, SC
07 May 2024